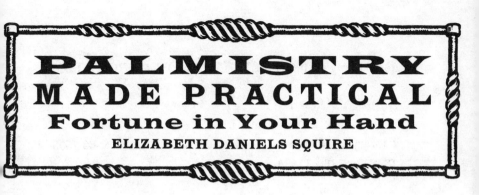

PALMISTRY
MADE PRACTICAL
Fortune in Your Hand
ELIZABETH DANIELS SQUIRE

Published by
Melvin Powers
WILSHIRE BOOK COMPANY
12015 Sherman Road
No. Hollywood, California 91605
Telephone: (213) 875-1711 / (818) 983-1105

Printed by
HAL LEIGHTON PRINTING COMPANY
P.O. Box 3952
North Hollywood, California 91605
Telephone: (213) 983-1105

Manufactured in the United States of America

CONTENTS

INTRODUCTION

"Consciousness of our powers increases them."
—Vauvenargues.

Why should you want to read hands? Probably you have picked up this book because you are curious about the kinds of things that are likely to happen to you—"what is my future?"

Perhaps you are interested in self-knowledge or in human nature or in patterns and symbols that appear in nature and art and were given special meanings by ancient religions and superstitions.

At any rate, if you take up the study of hands—beginning with your own—you will be opening the door to a number of intriguing corridors to knowledge. To begin, hand-reading can help you to know other people—and yourself, too.

A common first question may be about money: Are you likely to make a fortune on your own? Could you hold on to money if you inherited it? Or are you one of those persons to whom worldly possessions are not really very important? Do you have what it takes to attract "good luck"? Or will you always work hard for every advantage you gain? It's fascinating to check the readings in your hand against actual experience in the past, and then estimate the future.

If you are married, you may be surprised to find how much more you will know after reading your hands and your mate's—more about some of the ways you get along best, and more about some of the areas that invariably spark an argument.

If you are single, it may interest you to discover that many of the dates who attract you most have hands roughly alike.

Or your interests may be deeper and you may want to acquire enough self-knowledge to find more inner harmony. Reading many hands and seeing how your problems compare with other people's problems seems to help with that.

Also, if you make a study of hand-reading, you'll discover that even casual glances at the hands of new contacts will give clues about how best to approach each person.

If you want to win the support of someone with large hands and long, knotty fingers, you'd better have all the facts ready. He'll want to know the details and study the whole situation before he makes up his mind

If you've ever heard families discuss whether Willie or Mary takes after Mother or Father, you'll realize how much fun it can be to look at the hands and see what facets of character come from which side of the family. Sometimes a child's hands will differ from the hands of both his parents but will closely resemble the hands of a grandparent, aunt or uncle.

You can check any part of hand-reading against experience—for example, whether a child really behaves as much like a particular relative as his hand says he will.

While I doubt if anyone ever learned to read hands for self-protection alone, the fact is that learning to read hands is some protection against an amazing con game that is based on hand-reading. But more of that later.

I am not a mystic or a scientist but a reporter, and

the reader will find my attitude toward hand-reading is flavored accordingly. That is why I keep referring him back to his own first hand experience. With an art that has been used for centuries as a tool of folk psychology, his personal experience will be a more fitting guide than my recommendation. (That is not the only way hand-reading has been used and judged, but it is one common way.)

It strikes me as amazing that some people scoff at hand-reading without trying it or bothering to find out about it, and equally amazing that others believe in it without bothering to find out anything about it, even going to hand-readers they know nothing about and then believing every word these unknown readers say.

As a reporter, I have been as interested in finding out about ways that hand-reading is used as in practicing it. That has required talking to people with violently differing points of view. For example, I had lunch with a self-declared witch and interviewed a police detective in charge of tracking down fortune-tellers, all in the same day. My doctor lends me medical journals that mention the use of hands in medical diagnosis. I talk to hand-readers who practice for their own enjoyment, wherever I go.

Letters I received while I was writing a syndicated column about hand-reading were a gold mine of information, too. And I've enjoyed the lectures given by the American Society for Psychical Research, an interest-group that includes scientists, people who believe they have extra-sensory abilities and others who just plain want to know more.

I have always wanted to find out whether things connected with hand-reading that are said to happen really

do. After all, in life what is "supposed to happen" frequently does not.

One day, while helping to prepare a television script,
I analyzed hand-prints and photographs of hands, an
astrologer I had never met analyzed the birth-dates of the
same people, and a hand-writing analyst prepared a report on their hand-writing. Then we compared reports for
each subject. The reports were recognisably alike but not
so alike that it seemed as if one analyst might have copied
the other. Each enlarged on different facets of the personality. (There is, of course, more than one explanation
of how this could have happened: the skeptic would say
it was rigged; the ESP buff would say it was ESP; the
occultist would say it was to be expected.)

But this made me more interested in the early con-
nections among hand-reading, astrology, hand-writing
analysis and other arts that the traditional occulist used
jointly to judge a man.

That is not to say that the author of this book is
a member of an occult religion. I am not. And that brings
me around to a little-understood fact about hand-reading.
There are four distinct kinds practiced in America today,
each with a long tradition behind it. There is the occultist; the folk hand-reader, the member of a conventional
scientific discipline, and the con-game artist.

Because this division is not generally understood, all
hand-readers are generally assumed by the man in the
street to be occultists; well-meaning hand-readers are
amazed to find themselves arrested, while distraught
people who wander in to see unknown hand-readers to
ask for help are sometimes defrauded of their life's savings.

The member of an occult sect is practicing his religion
when he reads a hand, for he believes there is a religious

message in all natural patterns—notably the patterns of the stars, of the hands, of the whole body, of the handwriting, of taro cards laid out for the subject, and such. The beliefs of occult sects differ, but one belief seems to be common to all that I know anything about: An occultist would call this an oversimplification, I am sure, but in general he believes that the fact that natural patterns have interrelated meanings proves that the universe is not a product of chance but of a meaningful force—which is to say God.

There are evidences that religious hand-reading may have a very long tradition—that, in fact, it may have started in the Stone Age.

Some caves contain whole hand-prints that, perhaps, were left as a signature at a Stone Age religious initiation. Other hand-prints make it seem that some Stone Age men cut off finger joints and printed the record of this bloody sacrifice on cave walls.

Like the graceful prehistoric pictures of horses, bison, mammoth or woolly rhinoceros, hand-prints made with black pigment and red-ochre hand outlines can be seen in the cave of Atamira at Santillana del Mar, Spain, and in other European caves. Abbe Henri Breuil has written about these discoveries.

Some anthropologists believe Stone Age hand-mutilations and hand-printing were magic ritual, but because the cave men lived before written history, we still ask if cave magic or religion included hand-reading.

At any rate, methods of "reading" natural patterns—such as might be formed by lines on, and shape of, a hand—are as old as the oldest written records. (One place to find out about this is the 11th edition of the Encyclopaedia Britannica, under "Omens.") Clay tablets from the region near the Tigris and Euphrates rivers tell how priests in about 2800 B.C. read the livers of sacrificed animals to predict the future of King Sargon I by shapes and markings described as holes and paths, and by the position of these. Some of these "signs" are like those hand-readers study now.

And priests studied the patterns of the stars, and their star-reading led to later forms of astrology, whose language and ideas are still part of hand-reading. Today, palmists still name each part of the hand for a planet. For example the base of the thumb is the "Mount of Venus" and when it is large and rosy it is believed to reveal strong physical passion.

Certain designs had a similar meaning in more than one kind of early omen and in more than one part of the world. And certain favorable designs became charms to ensnare good luck. The circular line was meant to ensure good luck when it was used in a Babylonian or Hebrew devil-trap, for example, or an Egyptian ring amulet. Squares could be magically protective and were the true form for amulets among the Arabs and Persians and much used by other early peoples. (Many of these charms and omens are described by Sir E. A. Wallis Budge, of the British Museum, in his "Amulets and Talismans.")

The well-formed triangle was a good sign, seen for example in the shape of a torch flame or on a sacred bull amulet, or formed by the letters Abracadabra in an amulet to cure fever.

The out-of-the-ordinary mark or shape meant something remarkable for good or evil. The broken line signified the negative or passive, the unbroken line the positive or creative. (An example is the line-patterns used in the ancient Chinese book of changes, the I Ching.)

These same pattern-readings, and others equally ancient, are in recent hand-reading how-to-do-it-yourself books on my library shelf. A circle suggests you are creative; a square means protection; broken lines in your hand are read as negative signs (though no "sign" is read alone, and thus none is entirely negative or entirely positive). A clear and balanced triangle of the head, life and fate lines is still considered "lucky." A wild and out-of-the-ordinary pattern of lines is a sign of something out of the ordinary in your makeup and possibilities.

These ancient signs, incorporated in hand-reading, certainly appear to be graphic reminders of a religious and magical heritage. The occult hand-reader is sure they are. He also will often tie in his reading with philosophy based on reincarnation. He may mention a connection between hand-reading and the Kabbalah. The hand-reader gives the subject religious advice along with the reading.

Sometimes the religious hand-reader calls himself a scientist—and this can be confusing. He means to imply, I gather, that he considers he is more truly on the path to knowledge than the member of a scientific discipline with a conventional diploma from a university—the biologist, say, or a medical doctor.

It muddies the issue, however, because in addition to occult hand-readers who call themselves scientists, there are also conventional scientists who study hand-patterns. For example, the study of the pattern of the tiny papillary ridges on hands and feet is called "dermatoglyphics," and the patterns have been shown to vary to a statistically significant degree between different racial groups and between members of the same group who are subject to certain diseases. Dr. Ruth Achs and Dr. Rita Harper have found a line-pattern useful in diagnosing birth defects. As you'll see when you read the history of hand-reading, there

have always been doctors who used it for their purposes.
    The Journal of the American Medical Association has
pointed out that there is absolutely no connection between
the way doctors read hands and the way other hand-
readers work. While specific doctors may be interested in

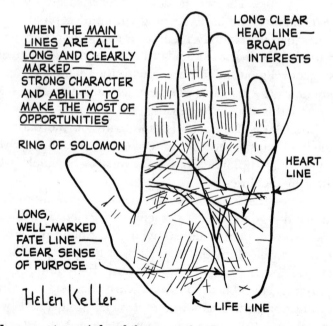

WHEN THE MAIN
LINES ARE ALL
LONG AND CLEARLY
MARKED —
STRONG CHARACTER
AND ABILITY TO
MAKE THE MOST OF
OPPORTUNITIES

RING OF SOLOMON

LONG,
WELL-MARKED
FATE LINE —
CLEAR SENSE
OF PURPOSE

LONG CLEAR
HEAD LINE —
BROAD
INTERESTS

HEART
LINE

Helen Keller

LIFE LINE

Here are signs of the ability to make the most of opportunities.
They belong to Helen Keller, who has led such a remarkably
useful and interesting life in spite of the fact that she can
neither see nor hear. (Original length of print 7-1/4 inches)

occultism, there is in general no love lost between scientific and occult hand-readers. Yet to the layman it seems that some of the doctors' discoveries and the occultists' readings are enough alike to be interesting, as you'll see. That the two kinds of students are very different in their aims, however, there's no denying.

The third kind of hand-reader is the kind I have always thought of as the "black" hand-reader—because the reader aims to misuse hand-reading just the way the black magician aims to misuse other occult arts. He is the hand-reader who makes the headlines when he is discovered and arrested. Black hand-readers use the same methods of fraud in all parts of the world, police report, and like the religious hand-readers they seem to have a long tradition. They usually call themselves religious hand-readers.

In the Middle Ages, for example, one of the men who contributed to the Faust story was a wandering European mountebank, sorcerer and doctor who owned a trained dog or horse and contributed to the legend of the man who sold his soul to the devil. He had studied magic at Cracow and he practiced all of the "occult" arts including hand-reading, ritual magic, astrology, divination, alchemy and necromancy. One story says he was finally strangled by the Devil.

Perhaps he was typical of the worst sort of wandering hand-reader, if more colorful than most. The legend of Faust became more formidable than the man himself, for in his own time he was often regarded as a drunken braggart and a quack.

Even earlier evidence of the misuse of hand-reading is in the warning against dishonest hand-readers in the Indian Laws of Manu, dating from around 100 B.C.

The first step in the dishonest hand-reader's ploy is

to win confidence by telling things that are true. The
black hand-reader's method of producing the impressive
truth is variously described. A detective told me she believed these readers used shrewdness to estimate character
and "played back" the information she let drop to make
the reading more convincing. After you have learned to
read hands, you may agree with my feeling that a good
hand-reader could tell quite enough in a perfectly normal
hand-reading to impress a gullible person, if he so desired.

At any rate, the black hand-reader implies that he has
second sight, that second sight can come only from God
and that therefore if he can "see" incidents in the past,
he must be honest. It might help a person faced with one
of these hand-readers to know that people who have
studied extra-sensory perception say there seems to be no
connection between honesty and E.S.P. Like intelligence,
E.S.P. falls to the honest and the dishonest alike. Also, in
my opinion, most hand-reading does not depend on E.S.P.
—that being a fringe benefit.

Once the black hand-reader had persuaded you he was
honest and had clairvoyant powers, he would say he could
"see" a curse on something you owned. This curse, he
would explain, caused all your problems. Then he would
ask you to bring him various objects you owned so that he
could test them to see which were cursed. If you had inherited money, it would eventually work out to be the
money that was cursed. To remove the curse, you would
have to allow the reader to burn the money. After you
drew thousands of dollars out of the bank, you could
watch while the reader put it in a burner and you could
watch the smoke rise. The reader would vanish before you
came to your senses and began to doubt if all that money
had really burned. A case of this sort involving more than

$30,000 got quite a play in the New York newspapers a few years ago.

In an alternate ploy, the money is "cleansed" by sewing it into a package or the lining of your coat for, say, six months. The reader would have vanished by the time the subject discovered she had old newspapers sewn into her coat. (The subject is usually a woman—a widow, to be exact.)

If these con-games seem too transparent to work, remember that panic can make the most sensible-seeming person do strange things. I'm always reminded of a family story about my great-grandfather who rushed into the house, yelled "Fire! Fire!" and hustled his family out, then grabbed a valuable glass vase he loved and threw it out the window to "safety."

The fourth kind of hand-reader on the scene today is the modern equivalent of the folk hand-reader of earlier days. The only difference is that the modern hand-reader generally learns the art, to begin with, from a book rather than from oral tradition. The book he uses has typically been compiled from several sources including older folk hand-reading, bits of information culled from medicine and other science, new and old, and material that is also a part of occult hand-reading.

This half-book-half-folk hand-reading has been practiced in America at least since sailors on early whaling ships took hand-reading books on their long voyages to while away the time between whales. For-pleasure hand-readers may read palms for a lifetime and are often excellent. Many tea-room hand-readers are for-pleasure hand-readers gone commercial.

I have, however, received sad letters from folk hand-readers turned professional who have been arrested because they predicted the future for a price in an area where they didn't know it was against the law. Others have been propositioned to do things they considered dishonest. They reported that shady types asked them to report "success in real-estate investments" or a quick profit in some worthless stock, then became quite abusive when the reader refused. Evidently, dishonest promoters had sometimes dealt with more cooperative hand-readers.

The best hand-readers, however, are honest and read hands because they are interested in people or because it is their religion.

This book has not been written to expound any one theory of hand-reading. It is meant to be a simply written and clearly and amply illustrated how-to book for beginners. Some hand-prints and photographs are marked with the degree of reduction, so that it is possible to know the original size. Hand diagrams are reductions of exact tracings of prints. Dotted circles show areas of high padding on some diagrams.

The advanced student will be interested in the hand-prints but will find parts of the text over-simplified, I imagine. I have therefore included a bibliography at the end of the book for the student who wants to learn more so that he can read about whichever facet of hand-reading interests him the most.

As for the theories, the names of the parts of the hand make one of these obvious—that the hand shows the influence of the stars.

Another, propounded by Dr. Charlotte Wolfe, a British psychiatrist, is that hands reveal the state of the ductless glands and other physical conditions that are related to temperament.

Old-time hand-readers believed that the lines in the

hand could not be related to the way people used their hands. Manual laborers or craftsmen, they noted, have far fewer lines in their hands than dreamers or intellectuals do.

Now scientists know that traces of movement accompany thought. If you think about playing the piano, for example, your fingers move slightly—so slightly it is not even noticeable. You undoubtedly know people who make grand gestures as they talk—but all of us make at least slight, subtle gestures as we think, whether we realize it or not.

So the hands of dreamers have hundreds of lines while those of the craftsmen are more likely to have few lines.

Other theories about why hand-reading works are mentioned in the history of the art that follows.

The interesting fact about all the many types of people who have been seriously interested in hand-reading and set forth theories about it is that they all agree on one thing: Hand-patterns are meaningful and well worth a careful study.

In order to enjoy this old art, the reader has only to remember two things: First, that markings in hands are simply signposts indicating a probable direction, and that hands change, so it is foolish and unkind to predict inevitable catastrophes; second, that a knowledge of the how-to of hand-reading will not of itself make the reader an occultist or a scientist.

Hand-reading can, however, be an absolutely fascinating and fruitful study. It is also an antidote for the modern pressures that make each individual feel like a mere unimportant number out of a series in a computer. Hand-reading highlights the fact that each person—like each snowflake, each plant, each individual creation in the world—is marvelously unique.

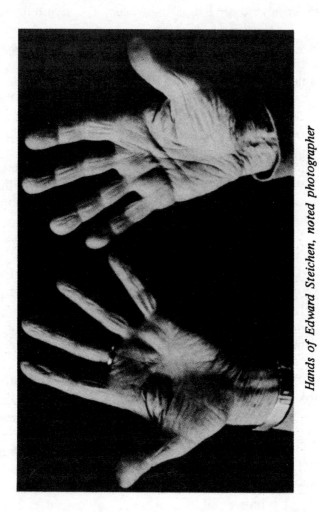

Hands of Edward Steichen, noted photographer

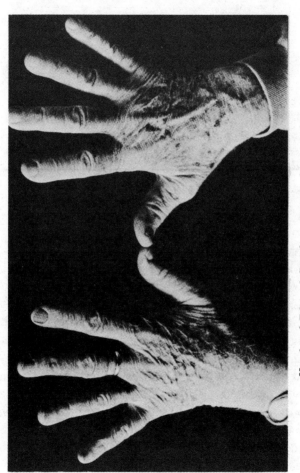

Hands of Edward Steichen, noted photographer

CHAPTER I

HOW IT ALL BEGAN

"There is nothing in the three worlds for knowledge besides the hand which is given to mankind like a book to read."

—Hastha Sanjeevan.

There are hints that some meaning may have been attached to the designs found on hands since pre-history. There are those hand-prints on cave walls, for one example, and designs that could be copies of finger-prints in a Stone Age burial passage on an island off Brittany, for another. Was hand-reading practiced by early man?

Hand-reading's earliest origins are embroidered by myth, legend and tradition. It probably began in India long before written history. Indian tradition holds that the art of divination by all the limbs of the body, or Anga Vidya, was handed down by Samudra, the Sea God. The study of hands and feet was the most important part of Anga Vidya.

Tradition also holds that when Buddha was born (about 563 B.C.) he had marks on his feet that enabled sages to foretell his greatness. And people believed that Lord

Krishna (an incarnation of Vishnu come to help men in their sufferings) had special markings on his feet and hands.

Even today, Hindu hand-readers believe the appearance of marks such as those on the hands or feet of Krishna or the Buddha foretell a great destiny.

K. C. Sen, an Indian palmist, identifies the earliest documents on hand-reading as ancient Sanskrit verses or *slokas*, jealously guarded and kept from the public eye by Brahmin families in India. Cheiro, the seer so famous at the turn of the century, wrote that he was allowed to look at one of these documents. It was, he said, written in ink as red as blood on animal skins yellow with age.

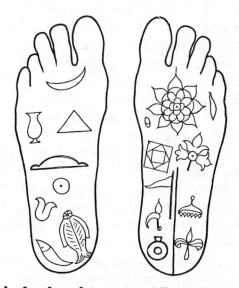

Marks on the hands and feet of Buddha in the sixth century B.C. made sages aware that he would be a great man.

One of the earliest records of Anga Vidya, or study of limbs, is in the Ramayana—an Indian epic poem about the adventures of a hero and the patient faithfulness of his wife. This epic, comparable to the Odyssey, began to take shape in the third century B.C. and was passed on by bards.

Early Indian hand-reading was closely linked to astrology or the study of the stars to determine human destiny. Hand-reading and astrology even have the same patron deity, Lord Skanda.

Possibly from India, hand-reading spread throughout the ancient East. Later it reached Asia Minor and entered Europe about the time of Alexander the Great.

Gypsies, who are palm-readers by tradition, trace their tribes back to a village in Northern India, and their language is about one-third Sanskrit. Although some modern Gypsies rely more on astuteness and clairvoyance than on any real science of hand-reading, their palmist tradition clearly goes back to ancient India.

Hand-reading was well-known in Greece during the fourth century, B.C., reign of Alexander. Though brave as a lion and ready to rush into the bloodiest battles, Alexander revealed his concern about his future by a tremendous interest in all methods of predicting it, including, of course, hand-reading. First of all, his sword-makers were Gypsies—always skilled metal-workers and as we have seen, fortune-tellers. And secondly, Alexander spent two years in India attempting to conquer that country.

Aristotle, the philosopher who was Alexander's tutor, was supposed to have found an ancient Arabic document on hand-reading, written in characters of pure gold, on an altar to Hermes. Legend has it that he gave this document to Alexander. Probably Aristotle wrote a treatise on

hand-reading because of Alexander's interest in the subject.

When Aristotle's hand was read for the first time, the
story goes, his pupils were shocked by all the signs of
weakness found in his hand. But Aristotle accepted the
reading as truthful. He told his pupils that the faults read
from his hands were the very ones he had struggled all his
life to overcome.

Although much that Aristotle wrote on hand-reading
may be lost, his book on physiognomy—including material on the shape, color and texture of the hands—is
available today.

Most early Western books on the meaning of hands
were parts of longer works on physiognomy, or the character and likely fate of men as revealed by the shape of
the whole body. We have preserved in the West almost
nothing written in ancient times about the lines of the
hand. However, as you will see, the shape and size of
the hands and fingers and the texture and color of the
hands are the key to accurate hand-reading—and the
reading based on lines must be tempered by the reading
of the whole hand.

Aristotle does mention the meaning of lines in the hand.
In *De Historia Animalium*, he says that long lines belong
to long-lived people but that short lines mean shorter
lives. He may even have written a special treatise on lines,
though we have no record of it.

Later writers, feeling that Aristotle's name was more
respectable than their own, tried to fill in the gaps in
the philosopher's known works by adding works of their
own that they attributed to Aristotle. For example, a fifteenth century German work, *Cyromancia Aristotelis*
(Ulm, 1491), is a fascinating document typical of a later

stage of hand-reading, though scholars do not attribute it to Aristotle.

Some of the oldest writings about hands are not directly concerned with lines and shape. Instead they are concerned with the idea that various parts of the body can reveal us for what we are. A wonderful document written by Melampus in 247 B.C. deals with the significance of the itching and twitching of various parts of the body. Without even stopping to think about it, we still associate certain characteristics with itchy fingers or twiddling thumbs.

Many intriguing passages in the Bible seem to refer to the idea that a man's likely fate may be shown in his hands. These passages also suggest that hand-reading was known in Old Testament days. For example:

—"Length of days is in her right hand; and in her left hand riches and honor." Proverbs 3:16.

—"He sealeth up the hand of every man; that all men may know his work." Job 37:7.

—"And he said, Wherefore doth my lord thus pursue after his servant? for what have I done? or what evil is in mine hand?" I Samuel 26:18.

Early physicians studied the whole man—mind and body—and therefore medical books sometimes included physiognomy as a way of determining a man's likely characteristics. Famous cures were sometimes based on a knowledge of a patient's mind and heart.

Erasistratus, an Alexandrian physician, was said to have cured a son of the King of Syria from a dangerous illness. The real trouble, Erasistratus decided, was that the youth was in love with one of his father's wives. The father proved to be so anxious to help in the cure of his son that he divorced his wife. The son married her in turn and was thereupon cured of his illness.

This frontispiece from a seventeenth century Latin book includes quotes from the Bible believed to endorse hand-reading. (Photograph courtesy of The Library of Congress.)

Galen of Pergamum, a second century physician to several Roman emperors including Marcus Aurelius, is said to have written about physiognomy, not overlooking, of course, a good deal of material about hands.

In contrast to India, where the lines of the hand were read from earliest times, the West in the second century entertained only a primitive idea of line-reading, regard-

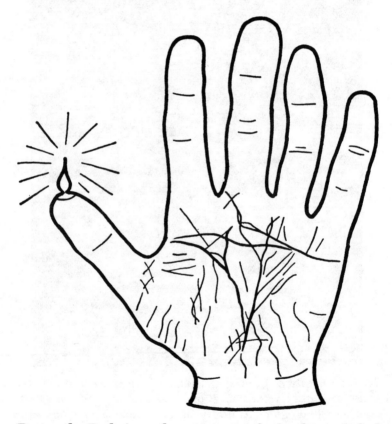

During the Dark Ages, the meaning of the hands was linked with black magic. Thieves lighted the thumb of a mummified robber's hand to paralyze their victim's will.

ing it as a form of divination. Juvenal said that in his day upper-class women consulted astrologers while middle-class women went to hand-readers.

TRADITIONAL WITCHES' HAND

Arab doctors were influenced by the Greek and Roman. In the eleventh century, Avicenna—an Arab physician—wrote about the meaning of the shape and form of the hand in his huge book, *Quanoun Fi ul-Tibb* (Canon of Medicine). Translated into Latin in the twelfth century, this became the most important text in European medical schools and was used in France as late as the mid-seventeenth century.

Along about the twelfth and early thirteenth centuries, interest in physiognomy and all forms of hand-reading spread throughout Europe. Johannes Hispalensis brought out a document, probably of Arab origin, that he believed to be an exact translation of the one found by Aristotle on the altar of Hermes. And when Thomas a Becket didn't know what advice to give Henry II about an invasion of Brittany, he consulted a chiromancer or line-reader.

Starting in the twelfth century, more and more manuscripts (though we have only fragments of the earliest ones) were written about lines and special signs in the hand. Until then, as we have seen, almost all Western writings preserved were about hand shapes and had nothing to do with lines. Most of the manuscripts about lines and signs are semi-magical and are hair-raising to read—an early substitute for the murder mystery.

Here, for instance, are some gloomy suggestions from a manuscript dated about 1400 A.D.:

"If several lines go from the life line toward the thumb, the owner will be killed or endangered by fire."

"If tangled lines rise from the hollow of the hand, ending below the middle finger, death in prison is indicated."

"If a figure like an 'e' is found near the bottom of the hand, the owner will kill his father or mother or despoil a holy church. A woman with this mark will be a common strumpet."

Interwoven with all this superstition was a grain of truth that was winnowed by later hand-readers.

I have not found any mention of the mounts, those areas of the hand that are often bulging like little hills, before the fourteenth century. But most histories of palmistry claim that the mounts were studied by the Greeks at the time of Aristotle. This, they explain, is because the Greeks were admirers of energy, symbolized by high, firm mounts.

Even today, the mounts are named for planets—another example of the close link between hand-reading and astrology.

In the fifteenth century, when the art of printing was still new, the first book on palmistry was published—a wood-block book by Johann Hartlieb called *Die Kunst Ciromantia.* Slightly later the manuscript signed "Aristotle" appeared, and was accepted until quite recently by students of palmistry as truly the work of the great philosopher. Dr. Hardin Craig analyzed many of the thirteenth, fourteenth and fifteenth century hand-reading texts when he was editing a fifteenth century book by John Metham for the Early English Text Society. His analysis shows that Aristotle gave only his name—and that, involuntarily—to *Cyromancia Aristotelis.*

Just as hand-reading was growing more popular in Europe, twelve Gypsy dukes went to work in Germany about 1414 as spies for Sigismund, the Holy Roman Emperor. At first, these Gypsy dukes and their tribes were considered fascinating and exotic with their wonderful romantic music, wild and beautiful dances and their ability to tell fortunes. The fortune-telling was, of course, a valuable tool in their real trades. By comparing the questions asked by a variety of people, the Gypsies could get a pretty clear idea of what was going on.

When a statesman's wife had a Gypsy hand-reading, her questions to the Gypsy could reveal her husband's plans. For example, "Does my hand show I could be faithful to my husband if he left me for a year?" Or, simply, "Does my hand show a journey?"

The dukes were leaders of a large group of Gypsies who wandered through Germany and Italy. Their spying was soon suspected. Rumors that they were not only fascinating but dangerous preceded them into France. They were light-fingered as well as light-footed. Worst of all, the Church felt they stirred up old pagan beliefs among the faithful.

When bands of Gypsies arrived at the gates of Paris in 1427, they were politely but firmly asked to remain outside the city at La Chapelle St. Denis. But the people of Paris, probably feeling that exotic and dangerous visitors were much more exciting than people who were merely exotic, came flocking out of the gates to have their fortunes told.

To counter the Church's warning that they were inspired by the Devil, the Gypsy fortune-tellers explained that the Devil was afraid of silver and the sign of the Cross. If you frequently made the sign of the Cross over their hands with silver, they said, you would be perfectly safe. Naturally, the Gypsies kept the silver.

Undoubtedly, Gypsies made hand-reading seem more glamorous for a time, especially when they grew prosperous. Few realized that their prosperity was due to their role as spies for Sigismund. After 1437, without Sigismund's protection, they were condemned and treated with contempt. They were considered no better than godless bands of wandering thieves who were supposed to devour their parents and steal other people's children. This is why you won't find Gypsies mentioned at all in most histories of hand-reading.

For centuries afterward, the art of hand-reading was associated with the Gypsies' blackened reputation. Laws passed against the Gypsies made it illegal in many places for anyone to read hands, and even today, New York, Connecticut and several other states and municipalities have laws making it illegal to accept payment for fortune-telling.

Partly because of the Gypsies and partly in spite of them, hand-reading became more and more popular in the Middle Ages. Paracelsus, a controversial wandering sixteenth-century doctor with an inquiring mind, became so interested in hand-reading that he ranked it high among the sciences and called it the mother of the arts.

Paracelsus associated hand-reading with astrology and believed that the hand revealed, in one compact map, the astral signs also shown by the whole body.

He insulted traditional doctors with great fluency, and collected recipes from folk-medicine and probably from his fellow-wanderers, the Gypsies. That made him unpopular with doctors in his own time, but he denied the conventional medical world the pleasure of consigning him to oblivion, for he became famous for initiating the use of chemical medicines. He was also the first to mention the relation between goiter in the parent and cretinism in a child.

Since Paracelsus was a doctor and an occultist interested in astrology and folklore, he combined the main traditions of hand-reading. He never wrote a book explaining his whole system of hand-reading, however—he merely described it as the system used by the ancients. There were many books written about hand-reading in Paracelsus' time and later, including those by B. Cocles, Johann Indagine, Richard Sanders and Johannes Praetorius.

It was said that of fifty-five persons for whom Cocles predicted sudden death, only two were ungracious enough to die slowly.

Probably because hand-reading was still regarded as suspect, Johannes Praetorius gathered as many quotes as he could from the Bible to adorn the frontispiece of his seventeenth century book.

Scientific interest in the hands continued too, and we learn from Julius Spier that chirology was part of the curriculum of the German universities of Leipzig and Halle from 1650 to 1730.

In most places during the eighteenth century, men lost interest in hand-reading. In his preface to Spier's book, *The Hands of Children,* C. G. Jung wrote that the "rise of the Natural Sciences and with it of rationalism in the eighteenth century were responsible for the contemptible treatment and defamation of these ancient arts (astrology and hand-reading) which could pride themselves on a thousand years of history."

The eclipse was temporary, and by the 1800s hand-reading once more gained stature in the eyes of some of Europe's greatest men. Napoleon had his hand read and gave his name to the extra long, large index finger of the power-seeker—the "forefinger of Napoleon."

Honoré de Balzac, whose novels show such a profound knowledge of human nature, felt that hand-reading was one of the best ways to unravel the intricacies of the human heart.

About the same time, Alexandre Dumas, father and son, were friends and boosters of Adolphe Desbarrolles, who became known as the father of modern palmistry.

Desbarrolles, called "The Father of Modern Palmistry," reads a hand in his studio in Boulevard St.-Michel, Paris. (Photograph courtesy of the Library of Congress.)

He included in his system of hand-reading some conclusions of his friend Capt. Stanislas d'Arpentigny, who had spent years studying the shapes of hands.

Desbarrolles read character, the past and the probable future from the hands, but he wasn't a fatalist. He felt a man might change the direction of his journey through life through will power or help from others. He read the hands of many of the famous men and women of his day, including Pope Leo XIII, Napoleon III and the Empress Eugénie.

Although he was not a trained scientist, Desbarrolles sifted the evidence of what really worked in hand-reading. He was also interested in all the other sciences of character-reading and wrote a book on graphology.

Meanwhile, scientists were interested in their own kind of hand "reading." Francis Galton was one of those who wrote about fingerprint types and studied inheritance and racial variation in fingerprints. Harris Hawthorne Wilder and others studied the tiny papillary ridges of palms and soles. These biological studies, so far from the Gypsy's tent or the occultist's study, were the beginnings of the science of dermatoglyphics—which has only lately thrown some light on one of the ancient "signs" that palmists called a warning of a miserable or untimely end. But more of this later.

Not skin-ridges but hand-shapes interested Carl Gustaf Carus, personal physician to the King of Saxony in the mid-nineteenth century. Carus thought that evolution accounted for different hand-shapes.

Two principal types of hands were identified by Carus —the purposeful hand, best adapted to grabbing or holding on, and the expressive hand that uses the sense of touch to explore and learn.

Just as Desbarrolles inspired later traditional hand-readers, Carus had a great influence on Charlotte Wolff, a modern-day physician and psychologist who has made a study of human character as revealed in the hands.

Another scientist who became interested in the application of scientific method to hand-reading was Dr. N. Vaschide, a member of the French Academy of Sciences. He, too, worked to put hand-reading on a scientific basis, but his reward was ironic. While Dr. Vaschide was engaged in research, a fortune teller foretold every detail of his tragic early death.

The most colorful name in late nineteenth century hand-reading was that of Cheiro (Count Louis Hamon). Cheiro's career extended spectacularly into the early part of the present century. When he was quite young, his mother, who was a student of palmistry, saw from her son's hand that he had a strong talent for the occult sciences.

The young Cheiro began to study his mother's copious collection of books and went on from there to become one of the world's greatest hand-readers. He also studied graphology, astrology and numerology and could predict in great detail the course a life would take.

Cheiro called himself a seer. He was undoubtedly clairvoyant as well as deeply versed in all the sciences and arts of knowing human beings.

Vii Putnam, granddaughter of King Michael of the Gypsies, tells me that Cheiro was half-Gypsy, though it isn't generally known in non-Gypsy circles. Here is her account: Cheiro's mother was from a wealthy Irish family and his father was a Gypsy count. He was sent to India to study when he was about fourteen.

A person of tremendous magnetism, Cheiro was elected King of the Gypsies. (The Gypsies have a hereditary nobility but elect their kings). Not wishing to rule, Cheiro "passed the ring," as the Gypsy expression goes, to the next most popular candidate.

Cheiro, because hand-reading was still associated with the kind of Gypsies who told fortunes by hook or by crook, chose to refer to himself as a Greek count rather than as a Gypsy of noble birth. His rise to success was not only due to his own great talent but also because the times were ripe for the appreciation of a "seer."

In the early part of the nineteenth century, Indian philosophy began to be translated into European languages. The Romantic writers, artists and philosophers hoped to find, in Eastern ideas, all the mysticism and mystery that had been logically argued out of existence in the West. There was a wave of translations of the sacred books and literature of the East.

In 1875, the Theosophical Society was started to promote a moral philosophy that combined Hindu mysticism with Christian morality. The society launched its own publishing firm, which published (among other titles) a widely read book on Indian hand-reading by Mrs. J. Dale.

Educated people with open minds began to study psychic phenomena such as mind-reading and clairvoyance. In England, the Society for Psychical Research was started in 1882—the forerunner of all the groups studying extra-sensory perception. William James, the psychologist, was a supporter of such research.

Cheiro, the "Greek" count—handsome, young, intelligent and truly clairvoyant—knew Annie Besant, a founder of the Theosophical Society. He knew Swami Vivekananda, the Indian philosopher. And he read the hands of many great personalities, including Gladstone, Mark Twain and later Douglas Fairbanks and Mary Pickford.

Cheiro knew William G. Benham, the great American hand-reader, and wrote him a letter of congratulation upon the publication of the latter's book, *The Laws of Scientific Hand Reading.* While Cheiro was a mystic, Benham approached hand-reading as a lover of logic.

Benham became interested in hand-reading when he was about thirteen years old, and as he learned, he talked to all the professional hand-readers he could find. He was amazed to discover that these professionals knew only a few rudiments of the art. So he worked out his own methods and theory of hand-reading, using these rudiments plus experience, before he found such books as the *Révélations Complète* of Desbarrolles.

Benham became so interested in why hand-reading worked that he studied some medicine. He was a man with the large thumbs that show force of character, and he kept exhaustive files and records of his work. He started a hand-reading school that is carried on by one of his pupils, Florens Meschter, in New York.

Other hand-readers of note near the turn of the century included the Comte C. de St. Germain, who founded the National School of Palmistry in Chicago; Katherine St. Hill, who started the Chirological Society in England and E. H. Allen, who translated d'Arpentigny's book on hand-shape types.

By an ironical twist, contemporary Indian hand-readers began to study the European system because it was more advanced than their own for character reading. K. C. Sen includes a bibliography in his book *Hast Samudrika Shasta* that lists more European than Indian titles.

Influence was not entirely one-sided. The ideas of Julius Spier, a "psycho-chirologist," resembled the Indian as well as the European system. He thought the hands showed the character of our ancestry. Some Indians believe the hand gives a clue to previous incarnations.

Spier obtained such amazing results from reading character and past experience from hands that he aroused the interest of C. G. Jung, pioneer psychologist. Jung, in his preface to Spier's book published posthumously in 1944, wrote that "I have had several opportunities of observing Dr. Julius Spier at work, and must admit that the results he has achieved have made a lasting impression on me."

"I found an excellent teacher in Julius Spier," said Dr. Charlotte Wolff, whose *Studies in Handreading* explained how she remained interested in hand-reading while she became a member of the British Psychological Society. "I was inspired to continue my studies in hand-reading," she said, "not only by the discoveries which had been made in the field of graphology, but also by the psychoanalytical works of Sigmund Freud and C. G. Jung. I tried to apply to hand-reading the newly found knowledge of the unconscious with the light it threw on dreams, imagination and art."

To those who feel that searching for any truth in conventional hand-reading is like opening a Pandora's box of superstition, even serious scientists who have studied hand-reading seem controversial and "far out." Exceptions to this rule are the doctors and other scientists involved in dermatoglyphics. This study of hand-markings, with emphasis on the tiny papillary ridges of the skin, is based on such thorough and widespread research—including study of the palms of apes and of racial samplings of *homo sapiens* from all over the world—that it has not been branded as controversial.

In fact, Dr. Ruth Achs and Dr. Rita Harper use dermatoglyphics in a Brooklyn, N.Y. hospital to spot hard-to-find birth defects in babies whose mothers have had German measles during pregnancy. Theirs is strictly medical hand-reading.

Traditional hand-readers have also used hand-reading to diagnose illness or physical defects. But predicting disease is hardly a safe sport for amateurs, since the power of negative suggestion might actually help to cause disease.

But studies of skin-ridges, both by conventional scientists and by hand-readers such as Noel Jacquin, in England, have suggested a connection between skin-ridge patterns and non-medical characteristics, too.

Hand-reading is far from a finished, cut-and-dried science. There are different schools of hand-reading and different ways of approaching it.

Dermatoglyphics is so entirely scientific that it expresses hand-patterns in mathematical formulas.

Another view is neatly expressed by Dr. Wolff:

"The psychology of the hand is like medicine, an art as well as a science; and accordingly intuition plays a part in it. But intuition must not be confused with clairvoyance."

On the other hand, clairvoyants have produced fascinating readings. A true understanding of what clairvoyance is and how it works may turn out to be one of the major scientific discoveries of our age because of research now being done by parapsychologists all over the world.

Clairvoyance is not yet sufficiently understood to be reliable; sometimes it works, sometimes it doesn't. One way to checking its accuracy is through hand-reading. Thus we can gain clues to what is likely to happen to a particular person.

The great advantage of hand-reading is that you don't have to be a clairvoyant or a scientist to learn the most valuable lesson it has to teach—a true understanding of human nature.

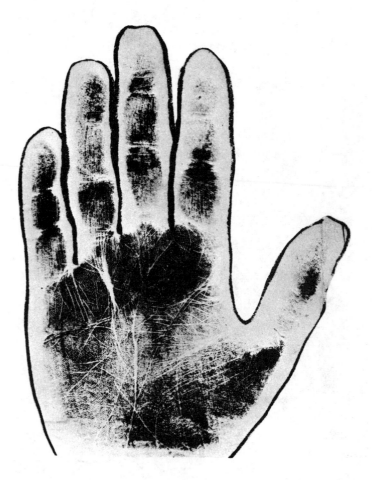

In general, inborn talents should be read from a right-hander's left hand . (Original length of print 7-3/4 inches)

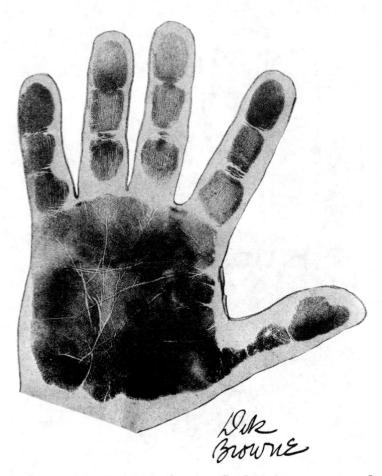

Dik Browne

Men whose work requires the same kind of temperament and talent tend to have the same general handshapes and types of line-markings. Compare this hand of Dik Browne, who creates the "Hi and Lois" comic strip, with that of cartoonist Charles Addams and that of comic artist Rube Goldberg.

(Original length of print 7-3/4 inches)

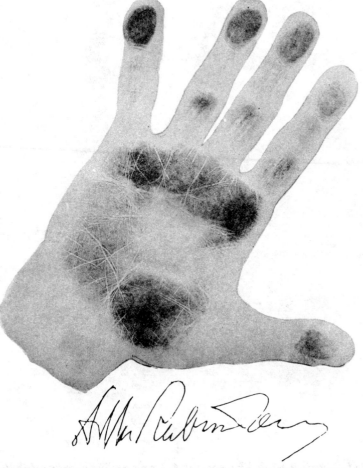

Artur Rubinstein took this print of his own hand without putting a pad under the center of the palm—which serves to show how high the padding tends to be on the hand of a musical virtuoso, so high that the lower areas in the center of the palm are difficult to print. (Original length of print 6-7/8 inches)

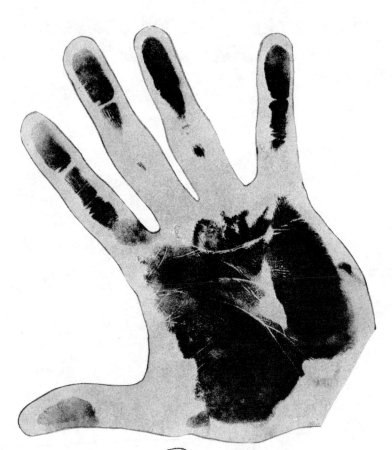

The musical hand like composer Dave Brubeck's has a highly developed Mount of Venus and Mount of Moon—thumb base and heel of hand. The knot, or pronounced joint, at the base of the thumb accompanies an excellent sense of rhythm. A naturally out-leaning little finger means a finely tuned ear.
(Original length of print 8-1/2 inches)

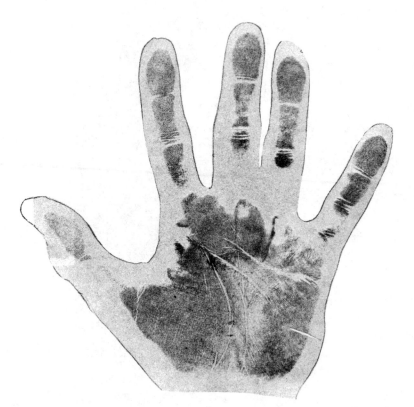

Producer David Susskind's hand is very firm, with a huge thumb and a well-marked verticle line up the center of the hand. If your hand is like this, you'll be continuingly successful —not through any fluke of good luck but because you are willing to work harder than most men can even imagine, in order to make the most of your talents. Note similarities with the hand of Patrick Dennis. (Original length of print 8 inches)

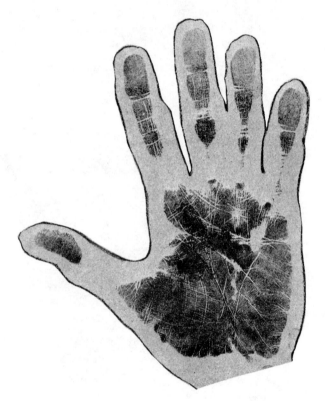

This hand shows an entirely different source of success. Moodiness, indicated here by numerous lines including some in grills on finger-mounts, can lend wonderful intensity and feeling to the work of a performing artist such as blues and folk singer Libby Holman. Often, the hands of famous people show that their most remarkable accomplishment has been to turn even their imperfections to advantage.

(Original length of print 7-1/2 inches)

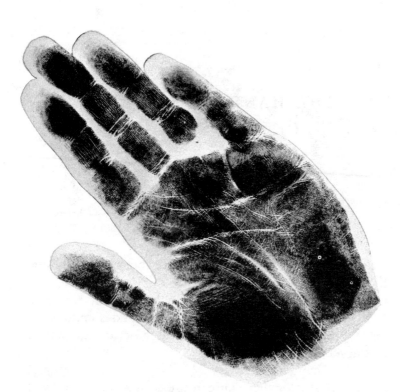

The hand with all fingers held close together and the thumb held up near the palm belongs to one who likes to hold onto the old, tried-and-true ways and doesn't really enjoy change. Add lines that are marked in a clear and balanced pattern. Then add head and life lines joined into one line for about an inch under the index finger. With this combination, you can expect a clear spokesman for the conservative point of view—and, in this hand of Russell Kirk, conservative columnist and author, you have it. (Original length of print 7-3/4 inches)

CHAPTER II

THE HAND AT A GLANCE
OR A HANDSHAKE

"The face allows itself to be too easily controlled to be accurate in its findings——."

—Cheiro.

To start with, you already know a lot about hand-reading, though perhaps you don't realize it. For instance, you would hardly disagree with the ancient Indian sage who made this shrewd observation: "The hand should have one thumb and four fingers, and if there are any more, it is a very bad sign."

In this chapter I've reviewed some of the more general signs of character that you can use to size up people you meet. See how many of them you already know:

The general position of the hand reveals the open or shut personality.

A tense person will clench his hands or hold them tightly shut. He is unusually inhibited and difficult to know.

If you hold your thumb over your fingers, prize-fighter fashion, it is a sign of belligerence or determination. But when you hold it tightly folded under the fingers as if it had to hide and the fingers needed something to hold on to, it indicates a fear of life and a desire to give up.

Tense hands usually accompany abrupt, awkward gestures, as any actor knows. And at the same time, tense hands may go with a smiling, self-assured face and are thus the only clues we have to the person's real state of mind.

Thumb clutched under fingers shows a desire to give up. The open hand belongs to an outgoing person. These pictures are from an eighteenth century French palmistry book. (Photograph courtesy of The Library of Congress.)

Not long ago, a young girl ran away from home on the eve of her marriage—evidently in a highly wrought state. Later, a magazine printed a smiling picture of the girl, taken a short while before she ran away, to show that she had given no outward signs of nervousness. In this picture, the face smiles—but the hands are desperately clenched.

At the other extreme is the open flabby, dangling hand

that represents a person lacking firmness of character or a strong sense of purpose. When you meet him, you feel as if you are shaking hands with a cold fish.

The firm, sure hand, more open than shut, belongs to the outgoing person.

The size of a person's hands gives an immediate clue as to how his mind works.

If a person's hands are out of proportion to the rest of his body, look for something original or even bizarre in his character. Notice how many pictures of monsters have hands out of proportion to the body.

The hand that is in proportion to the rest of the body is about the same length, from the wrist to the tip of the longest finger, as the face.

Very small hands show immaturity. Small hands reveal a childlike quality—often charming—and a mercurial temperament. For this reason perhaps, small hands also indicate a wish to do things in a big way.

Large hands belong to analytical people and, curious as it seems, those who can do delicate, detailed or intricate work. Have you ever wondered why so many dentists have large hands?

The general shape of the hand gives a quick clue to the sort of person with whom you're dealing.

Practical people with a good deal of drive and physical energy usually have broad, muscular hands. People who have nervous energy and a more inward turn of mind have narrow hands. You'll recall that many of the saints in famous paintings have long, narrow hands to emphasize the importance of the inner life. This doesn't mean all people with long, narrow hands are saints, however. Some are pickpockets.

Artists almost always use the appropriate hand-type to show character in a painting.

It seems obvious that graceful hands symbolize a greater inner balance than clumsy ones. Brilliant people may have awkward hands, but clumsy, lifeless-looking hands usually indicate a lack of brilliance.

The hand with firm, high padding belongs to the person

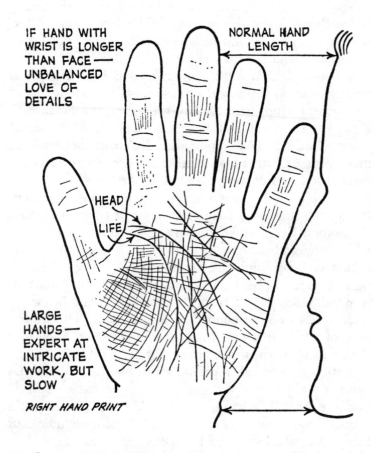

IF HAND WITH WRIST IS LONGER THAN FACE — UNBALANCED LOVE OF DETAILS

NORMAL HAND LENGTH

HEAD

LIFE

LARGE HANDS — EXPERT AT INTRICATE WORK, BUT SLOW

RIGHT HAND PRINT

Hand from wrist to longest fingertip is normally the same length as the face.

with lots of drive and a sure sense of his own abilities. It has been called the "lucky hand."

A flat hand belongs to the less confident person who has to work harder for what he gets. This doesn't mean he isn't talented and successful—merely that he has to work. But he has the energy to work, if his hand is also firm.

The thin, hollow hand—sunken like a bowl in the center but without high padding around the edges—is characteristic of the person who feels constantly defeated by bad breaks and who lacks the spirit to fight back.

A person with a solid, hard hand has lots of physical energy. And, as you might expect, a soft and spongy hand shows just the opposite. However, the man or woman with a soft hand and a large thumb may have plenty of mental energy, and this is a combination found in the hands of many persons with a high level of intellectual accomplishment. Eleanor Roosevelt has hands like these.

A flexible hand means a flexible mind capable of changing quickly from one train of thought or course of action to another. By "flexible," I don't mean to imply a lack of will or determination.

In a very flexible hand, the fingers can be bent back at right angles to the hand itself. Such are the hands of Alexander King. And many women lean their heads on their hands so as to bend their fingers back. They're the ones of whom it is said that "a woman's mind is cleaner than a man's because she changes it more often."

A stiff hand reveals a person set in his ways. When the hand is really stiff, the fingers won't bend back at all. If you've ever shaken hands with an old-time New England farmer, you know the sort of hand I mean (excluding, of course, the hand stiffened by disease or accident).

A skin as fine as a baby's suggests a delicately tuned person with hi-fi sensitivity. A coarser skin means an earthier person. Very coarse skin, as tough and wrinkled as the feet of a chicken, suggests a very coarse person— the kind for whom they invented "No Spitting on the Floor" signs.

Distorted, unbalanced looking hands show an odd original mind. But before you jump to conclusions, remember that an odd mind might belong to a genius or a crank. George Bernard Shaw had such hands.

The outwardly balanced hand reveals inner balance.

The color of your hands may depend on the temperature of the room or a temporary mood. But when you notice a pair of deathly pale hands in a warm room, you can assume the person is suffering from anxiety or an illness. Hands that are not a "sick white" but merely pale indicate a lack of energy, or egotism. Pink hands go with a warm and happy nature. Reddish hands are the sign of an optimistic, ardent, intense and, sometimes, irritable nature. Yellowish hands indicate a nervous person who is inclined to brood.

Your health and moods affect the temperature of your hands. If you have a fever, your hands are hot; when you are fearful or anxious, your hands are cold. We've all heard the expression "he got cold feet." When a man has "cold feet," he also has cold hands.

If you already know these clues to character, you undoubtedly have a natural knack for hand-reading. If you haven't been looking for these easy clues, pick them out and see how much more you can learn, at a glance or a handshake, about your fellow human beings.

Though these clues are easy, they are important. Remember them as you learn the more technical parts of hand-reading.

CHAPTER III

HOW TO MAKE A MAP
OF YOUR OWN HAND

"You cannot clap hands with one hand."
—Chinese Proverb.

The easiest and most interesting way to read your own hands is to make hand-prints and then mark them according to your character and possibilities, as you discover them. This is the professional way to read other people's hands. Here is how it is done:

Use a red office stamp pad—not the sponge-rubber kind but the old-fashioned cloth-covered type. You'll also need a soft pencil and six or eight sheets of smooth white paper, typewriter size—the smoother the better.

Start with a clean, dry hand. Ink a quarter of your hand at a time on the red stamp pad, using a corner of the pad to ink the hollow in the center of your palm. Ink your fingers too. Place your hand firmly in a natural position in the center of a piece of paper and *leave it there* while you trace your hand, fingers and thumb with the pencil. Be sure to hold the pencil straight up while you make your outline of each hand.

If the center of the palm doesn't leave a print, make

another hand-print with a folded handkerchief under the center of your palm. Continue making hand-prints until you get at least two good prints of each hand.

To obtain the best results, make those hand-prints now before you read the rest of this chapter. Check the finished prints against your hands to be sure they show the correct shape and all lines show up clearly.

Now you're ready to read the "map" of your hand. You will notice that you naturally put your hand down each time in approximately the same position so that your fingers are the same distance apart. Here's how hand-readers interpret the position of your fingers:

—When all your fingers are close together, it indicates that you are cautious and conventional.

—If your fingers are wide apart so that your hands look like a starfish, your mind is quick and flexible.

—If your index and middle fingers are separated, you are an independent thinker.

—If your middle and ring finger are separated, you are basically unconventional.

—If your ring and little finger are separated, it means you are free in your actions and decisions.

Any finger that seems to draw the other fingers toward it like a magnet gives a clue to a quality that dominates your life. In general, if the other fingers lean toward the ring and little fingers, your life will be molded more by emotion and instinct. But if your index finger and thumb seem to draw the other fingers toward them, conscious effort will guide you. This latter hand-position indicates leadership.

In a serious, conservative hand, all the fingers lean toward the middle finger. If your fingers don't lean at all but appear spaced, yours is a balanced personality.

You can learn a lot about yourself from observing the

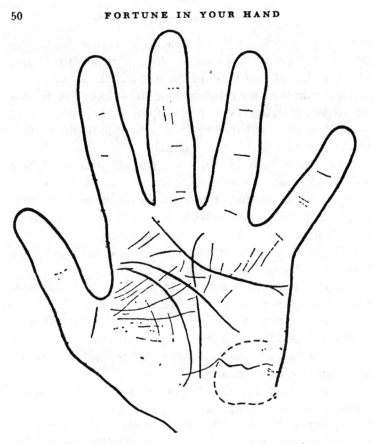

Your life will probably be guided by emotion and instinct if your fingers lean toward the little-finger side of the hand.

natural position of your fingers. Do you hold your little finger apart from its neighbors (freedom of action) and the index finger close? Perhaps you have Latin instincts and a Puritan conscience.

If your thumb is close to the fingers, you are probably a timid soul. But if it shoots out from the base of your hand and bends sharply in at the top like a claw, you are

DO YOU USE YOUR TALENTS?
— PATRICK DENNIS

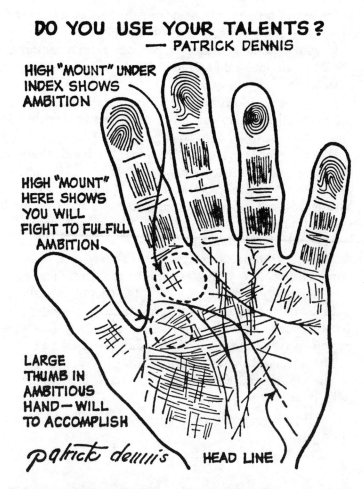

HIGH "MOUNT" UNDER INDEX SHOWS AMBITION

HIGH "MOUNT" HERE SHOWS YOU WILL FIGHT TO FULFILL AMBITION

LARGE THUMB IN AMBITIOUS HAND— WILL TO ACCOMPLISH

patrick dennis   HEAD LINE

Conscious effort will likely mold your life if the fingers lean toward the index and thumb. This, plus other features, shows deliberate good use of natural talent.

supposed to be a rapacious or greedy person. Witches are often pictured with a thumb of this kind.

If your thumb is widely separated from your fingers, you have an open mind. If held close, you are cautious.

In large and important ways the hands are almost always the same. Both hands will be broad with few lines —the hands of action—or both may be narrow with many fine lines—sensitive, high-strung hands.

When it comes to details, however, the hands are never the same. The most-used hand, left or right, is the hand that shows your ordinary workaday abilities and feelings. The least-used hand shows subconscious motives, undeveloped potentialities, or faults that have been controlled.

The old saying that the left hand shows qualities you were born with and the right hand shows what you have done with these qualities is close to the truth. The saying errs, however, in failing to take into account the fact that both hands change. As you grow and live longer, your potentialities and long-term desires change just as surely as your ways of dealing with life, day by day.

The left hand shows natural leanings.

The right hand shows how you have learned to deal with your life.

Whatever shows in *both* hands is 100% you.

LEFT HAND PRINT SHOWS WHAT YOU ARE BASICALLY

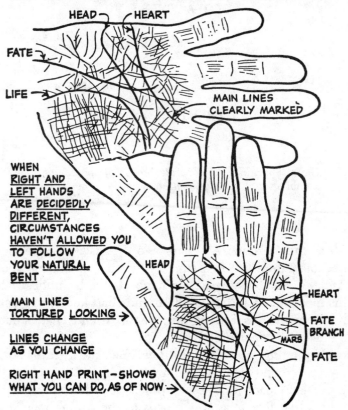

HEAD

HEART

FATE

LIFE

MAIN LINES CLEARLY MARKED

WHEN RIGHT AND LEFT HANDS ARE DECIDEDLY DIFFERENT, CIRCUMSTANCES HAVEN'T ALLOWED YOU TO FOLLOW YOUR NATURAL BENT

MAIN LINES TORTURED LOOKING →

LINES CHANGE AS YOU CHANGE

RIGHT HAND PRINT — SHOWS WHAT YOU CAN DO, AS OF NOW →

HEAD

HEART

FATE BRANCH

MARS

FATE

If the main lines are not clearly marked in the most-used hand (in this case, the right), there are obstacles that have hindered development of your abilities.

CHAPTER IV

HAND TYPES

"These types, like the separate breeds of the canine race, cannot alter or modify themselves beyond a certain point."
—Stanislas d'Arpentigny.

More than a hundred years ago, Stanislas d'Arpentigny became interested in palmistry when a beautiful young Andalusian Gypsy read his hand. Later he noticed that his mechanical and scientific friends had knotty or square hands while his artistic and poetic friends had smooth hands with tapering fingers.

Continuing his studies, he developed the idea that there are basic hand types which are related to basic character types—and each of these types is so different from the others that like separate "breeds of the canine race" they can't be altered beyond a certain point.

D'Arpentigny's classifications are used in modern hand-reading, though some changes have been introduced. Here are the principal types:

THE CLUMSY HAND

Since you can read this book, you may assume that yours is not an elementary hand that goes with a primitive and undeveloped intelligence. You can recognize such a hand not only by its clumsy shape but its hard skin, stiffness and the few lines that are more like creases in the skin than actual lines.

You might think that hands like this are the result of manual labor. But hands that work hard year after year become calloused—never clumsy.

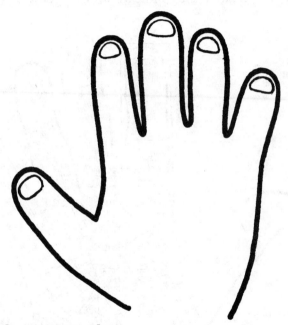

The Elementary Hand.

THE SQUARE HAND

Usually a broad hand with firm muscles, fingers of a rectangular shape and a square palm belongs to the decisive and active person whose thinking is down-to-earth. Such a person prefers to stick to tried and true traditions and customs until concrete examples convince him that new ideas or methods are worth trying. He has no respect for theories until he's seen them work. A farmer with square hands has no respect for new-fangled methods. An architect with these hands will prefer to design functional houses.

When fingertips are square (almost like a squared-off two-by-four board) they indicate an exaggerated love of

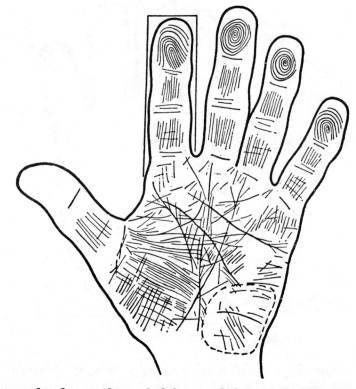

Square hands may have slightly rounded fingertips, but the fingers themselves are rectangular. The owner wants to know the truth, is often a scientist.

form. These very square tips are characteristic of builders and sometimes sculptors and architects.

The square hand is also called the "useful" hand because square-handers prize this quality the most in a person or object. These people are often too literal-minded. A boy shouldn't give a square-fingered girl a book of poetry but something she can wear or eat.

Fingers on a square hand are rectangular from base to tip, and the four sides of the finger are slightly flattened so that a cross-section would be square as well. The palm is generally square but the sides are not straight as a ramrod. In fact, the outer edge usually protrudes.

THE SPATULATE HAND

Perhaps your hand is more spatulate or flared. In its extreme form, this hand has what you might call stubbed fingertips that flare out at the tips like the spatulas used by chemists. The palm has an unusual shape—either the top of the palm or the bottom is broad, out of proportion to the rest of the hand.

This hand belongs to a person who combines a need for constant action with an original way of thinking. Such people are explorers of places or ideas. A dress designer with spatulate hands would be the one whose creations make you turn around and gasp. A general with spatulate hands would win battles because his strategy would take the enemy by surprise.

You will notice a hand that seems to be halfway between the extreme spatulate and the square. These hands belong to people who are original in a concrete down-to-earth way—often craftsmen whose work has great originality, tailors, for example. A writer with hands like this writes specifically, with many examples. The hands of such artisans may be nearly the same shape as square hands, and the flare in the fingertips is wider halfway up than at the extreme tip.

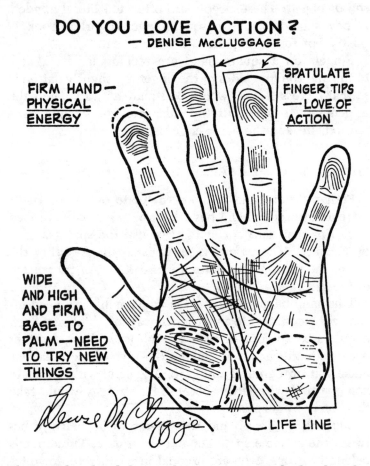

DO YOU LOVE ACTION?
— DENISE McCLUGGAGE

FIRM HAND—
PHYSICAL
ENERGY

SPATULATE
FINGER TIPS
—LOVE OF
ACTION

WIDE
AND HIGH
AND FIRM
BASE TO
PALM—NEED
TO TRY NEW
THINGS

LIFE LINE

The spatulate hand denotes love of action. If the hand is also firm and highly padded, this love of action is a consuming passion, as it is with woman sportscar racer Denise McCluggage.

If you have a spatulate hand, be careful to use your originality in a constructive way; otherwise you will become a crank.

THE PHILOSOPHIC HAND

If your hand is philosophic, it is long and bony with knots at both joints of the fingers. The palm, which is fairly flat, usually contains many lines.

The person with a hand like this wants to examine every

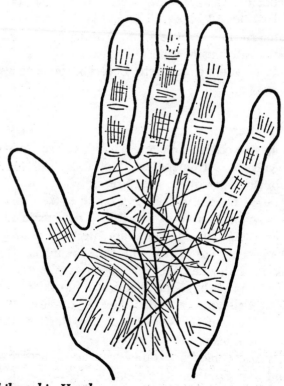

The Philosophic Hand.

side of a question before he makes up his mind. Ask him a question he does not expect, and he'll answer, "Well— yes and no."

Although the man with the philosophic hand feels he is searching for the truth, he is contradictory and difficult to understand. However, he understands other people, and though he is reserved, he is usually tactful. He needs to get off by himself to enjoy the peace of solitude. He loves the quiet countryside and long hours of uninter- rupted reading.

When this person makes up his mind to do something, he's as tenacious as a snapping turtle. He may stop to take another look at all sides of a problem, but then he'll start again. He has a restless and curious mind, and he's sometimes suspicious of others.

He likes to add up concrete, observed facts to get an abstract answer.

THE CONIC HAND

If you have a conic or receptive hand, you're a person to whom beauty is a tremendous inspiration. You're also a very impulsive person, a creature of whim and fancy. Conic-handed people will always try to make everything they touch as attractive as possible. Their main fault is that they would rather think about the ideal possibilities of life than face up to reality. But they are generally good companions, and when they are inspired, they are filled with infectious enthusiasm. They are fun to have at a party though they are not likely to stay to clean up. One warning to those of you who are conics: don't start more than you can finish.

Fingers in a conic hand taper to cone-shaped tips and are round like candles. The palm is slightly oval. Cleo-

ARE YOU BRILLIANT?
—ALEXANDER KING

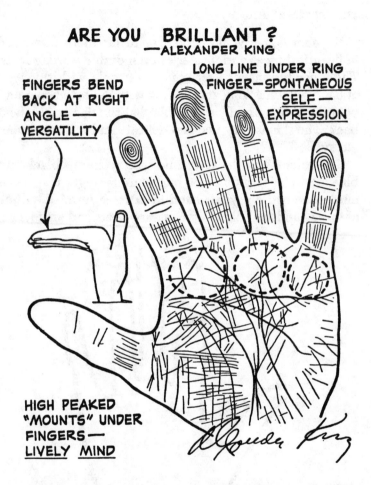

FINGERS BEND
BACK AT RIGHT
ANGLE —
VERSATILITY

LONG LINE UNDER RING
FINGER—SPONTANEOUS
SELF —
EXPRESSION

HIGH PEAKED
"MOUNTS" UNDER
FINGERS —
LIVELY MIND

A conic hand belongs to a versatile person, easily inspired but without much persistence unless he has large thumbs. Other hand features shown here may enlarge on versatility.

patra probably had hands like these. Conic hands usually have small thumbs (when they have large thumbs, their owners find it easier to finish what they start).

THE PSYCHIC HAND

If yours is a psychic hand, you're far more interested in beautiful ideas and mysteries than drab everyday facts. The inner life means everything to people with this type of hand, which is long and narrow with delicate bones and pointed fingers usually so flexible that the tips can be bent back. The skin is very fine and delicate and it is sometimes glossy.

The princess in the fairy tale who woke up black and blue after sleeping on a pea buried under eight mattresses must have had a psychic hand in extreme form. We think of these hands as belonging to saints, poets and aristocrats,

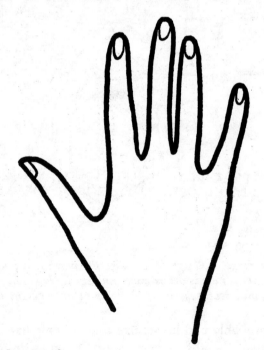

The Psychic Hand.

but this isn't necessarily so. A saint with such hands would put more emphasis on faith than works.

THE MIXED TYPE

Unless your hand happens to be a "pure" type, which is rare, you have to be satisfied with the designation "mixed type." The person with a mixed hand, however, is more

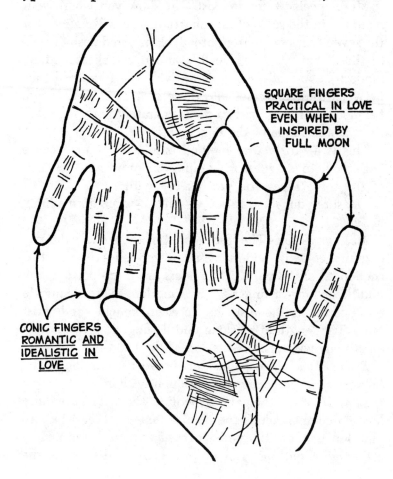

SQUARE FINGERS
PRACTICAL IN LOVE
EVEN WHEN
INSPIRED BY
FULL MOON

CONIC FINGERS
ROMANTIC AND
IDEALISTIC IN
LOVE

versatile than the man or woman with "pure" hands. You have probably already decided that the trouble with these various labels is the lack of specific tests or measurements to determine exactly your type or mixture of types. Experienced hand-readers can spot the elements of hand type in a mixed hand, but there is a need for more scientific measurements.

More specific tests do exist that show you where your hand fits in the scale of classification. You will notice that the seven types range from broad, clumsy and fleshy hands to those that are long, flexible and over-delicate. Many modern hand-readers prefer to divide the types of hands between these extremes into three simpler classes, broad, balanced and long, and to deal separately with such features as the shape of the fingers, etc.

This is a satisfactory method of classification because with the help of a measuring tape, you know exactly which of the three types you are dealing with.

Measure your hand to see whether it is broad, medium, or long.

Medium Hand—The width of the palm (half the circumference at its widest point) is very slightly less than the length of the palm. The fingers are in proportion—the middle or longest finger is the same length from knuckle to fingertip as the distance between knuckle and wrist bone. The length of the long middle finger approximately equals the width across the top of the hand.

Broad Hand—The palm is as broad as it is long. The fingers are in proportion and frequently short.

Long Hand—If the palm is medium, the fingers are quite long by comparison. If the palm is long or at least half an inch longer than it is wide *(curved measure),* the fingers are either slightly long or *in proportion* to the rest of the hand. In these hands, the fingertips are often longer than the other two sections of the finger.

THE BROAD HAND

If your hand is broad rather than long, you have the necessary drive to finish what you start. Your watchword

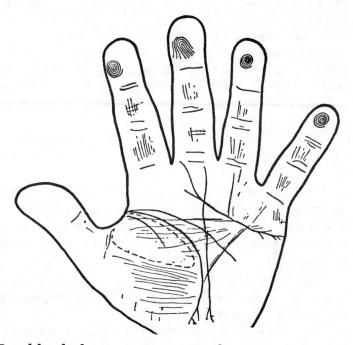

Broad hands show an active, practical nature.

is common sense; you enjoy luxuries and work to get them. Your feelings are quickly aroused, but you are inclined to be steady and true. Your thinking is practical.

If your broad hand is quite small, you are at once practical, mercurial and imaginative.

If your broad hand is very firm, you love nature and would prefer an outdoor job.

If you wish to use your imagination in a practical way, your hand is firm and broad with many signs of imagination. The politician who makes a heart-rending appeal to the voter has a hand like this.

If you have a broad hand that is very soft, you love comfort more than action. You prefer strawberry shortcake to football.

If your broad hand is unusually pale, flabby and soft, and has fingers that are fleshy at the base but taper considerably toward the tips, you are a lover of physical comfort but not an advocate of common sense. You are a sensualist or a dreamer or both. Swindlers often have hands like this, usually dead white.

NARROW AND LONG

If your hand is narrow and long, you have a more thoughtful and inward turn of mind—though if your hand is also strong and firm, you may have as much drive and sometimes more determination than your broad-handed friends.

Long hands go with inquiring and sensitive minds. These hands usually belong to expressive people, especially if the hands are also flexible.

Narrow-handed people are inclined to be shyer than broad-handed ones, however. Their thinking is abstract or imaginative, and they are more sensitive. If you are going to insult someone, pick someone with a broad hand. The broad-handed person may punch you in the nose, but the long-handed person will be more deeply hurt and will remember and resent the hurt long after the broad-handed person has forgotten it.

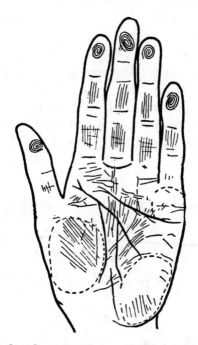

Long, narrow hands go with a reflective, often introverted, mind.

The long, slender hand can be as materialistic as the broad hand, though not in a comfortable way. If the hand is tense, stiff, thin, dry, knotty and curves inward, look for other signs of miserliness. If it is very white or yellow and has a bent little finger, you should suspect envy and the desire for concrete possessions to bolster the ego.

The balanced hand shows a balanced temperament. The size helps us understand the subject.

The size of the hand is an important measurable clue to personality. Hands of average length are about seven and a half inches long, excluding the wrist. Men's hands may be slightly longer, women's hands slightly shorter.

THE SMALL HAND

A definitely small hand would be less than six and three quarters inches long (Gertrude Lindsay says less than a Size 6 glove for women). A hand under seven inches would be small on a man. If you are under twenty, your hand may be small because it is not full grown.

Does the size of the person make a difference? If his

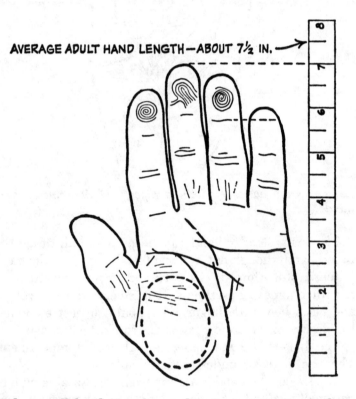

AVERAGE ADULT HAND LENGTH—ABOUT 7½ IN.

With a small hand (7 inches or less for a man, size 6 glove or less for a woman), you think vividly, like to make big plans.

hand is out of portion, his personality is not balanced. The distance from the wrist to the tip of the middle finger should be the same as the length of the face. (Look out for receding hairlines—they throw this measurement off.)

THE LARGE HAND

Very large hands belong to people who are willing to be patient with small details and can do very intricate work. They are analytical and thrive on details. The next time you visit your watch-repairman, study his hands. People with excessively large hands are moody.

If you have small hands, you are likely to have more charm than depth and more cleverness and perception than stick-to-itiveness. You do anything well that can be done quickly or on the spur of the moment, but you become exceedingly bored with any job that is long and routine. You would love to plan a church fair but hate to account for all the money that is made. You love to make plans but prefer that others carry them out. You succeed most often through the quick sale but fail when you lose interest in a job before you finish it.

You nearly always see signs of imagination in a small hand. Many writers have small hands. Thus they can visit a foreign country for two days and then write a five-hundred-page book about their "impressions." They think quickly and intuitively, almost never analytically. The person with small hands seems precocious in childhood and young for his age in later life.

THE BROAD SMALL HAND

The small hand that is broad and firm is energetically vivid and impulsive. People with these hands are often artistic and carry out their plans better than folks with narrow, small hands.

The person with broad, small hands with conic fingers is impulsive and imaginative, though if his hands are soft he is indolent and a lover of luxury.

If your hand is narrow and small, it is even more intuitive than the broad small hand. You are usually so high strung you must be careful not to wear yourself out.

Balanced hands that are neither large nor small show a balanced nature, but the fingers tell us about personality and character.

THE FINGERS

It is sometimes difficult to classify the various types of fingers. Are they square with conic tips and just a hint of spatulate flare? Unless they are clearly spatulate, conic, pointed or square, you had best determine whether they are tapered or rectangular.

SQUARE FINGERS

Place your hand on a sheet of paper with your fingers close together. Make an outline of your whole hand. Now draw a line parallel to your little finger and another line parallel to your index finger. If these lines form two sides of a possible rectangle, your fingers indicate that you are a practical, matter-of-fact person. If your hands show other signs of imagination, you may be artistic, though you require symmetry or realism in your art. Even if the tips are slightly rounded, these square fingers on a broad, firm hand show an extreme love of the functional and utilitarian.

Square fingers on a long hand mean that a person is

more sensitive and thoughtful but still basically practical. He will express himself clearly more than inspirationally. Scientists frequently have square fingers.

If the little finger line and the index line slope together slightly, the fingers are still predominantly of the square type.

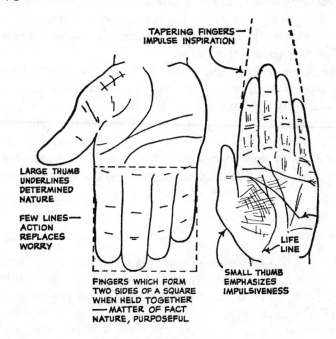

TAPERING FINGERS—
IMPULSE INSPIRATION

LARGE THUMB
UNDERLINES
DETERMINED
NATURE

FEW LINES—
ACTION
REPLACES
WORRY

FINGERS WHICH FORM
TWO SIDES OF A SQUARE
WHEN HELD TOGETHER
—MATTER OF FACT
NATURE, PURPOSEFUL

LIFE
LINE

SMALL THUMB
EMPHASIZES
IMPULSIVENESS

RECEPTIVE FINGERS

If your little finger line and the index finger line slope together quite noticeably, your fingers are receptive and you are an imaginative, often idealistic person.

On a broad hand these receptive fingers emphasize the enjoyment of all physical pleasures. If a person with such a hand wrote poetry, he would just as soon write an ode to a roast beef as a violet. People who love to cook usually have broad hands with receptive fingers, and such people are both less practical and more imaginative. They are not ethereal, however—they like their material comforts too much.

Receptive fingers on a long, slender hand indicate an appreciation of art, music, color and the beauties of nature. People of this type are otherwise less sensual in tastes than their broad-handed cousins. They would rather smell a rose than a roast beef.

The shape of your fingertips has a modifying effect on the shape of your hands and fingers. Square tips always indicate a love of form. Conic tips mean a bonus dash of idealism. Pointed tips are a sign of inspiration. Spatulate tips on any shape of hand indicate a love of activity and exploration of new places and ideas. On many hands the fingertips are not all the same shape. I will shortly explain the meaning of the shape of the tip of each finger.

FINGER LENGTH

The length of your fingers is also important. As I have pointed out, the average finger length makes the middle finger from tip to knuckle the same length as the back of the hand from knuckle to wrist.

SHORT FINGERS

Shorter fingers belong to people who think quickly and are impatient with details. Short fingers with smooth joints are characteristic of people who see the whole and have little patience with the parts. Fast thinking is their greatest asset. On the other hand, they often get into hot water by jumping to conclusions. If you are working from a palm

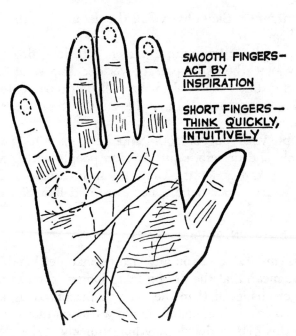

SMOOTH FINGERS—
ACT BY
INSPIRATION

SHORT FINGERS—
THINK QUICKLY,
INTUITIVELY

print, it is usually safe to class fingers as "short" if the middle finger is more than an inch shorter than the palm. However, this is not as accurate as measuring the backs.

LONG FINGERS

People who think in an abstract or analytical manner have long fingers. They like to go into details before they make up their minds.

They will read every word of a petition before they sign it. Particularly long fingers indicate such an extreme love of details that the whole picture is entirely lost. Those with extremely long fingers judge other people by details of manner and dress and are extremely meticulous. If their fingers have knots at the joints, they are more analytical.

Not only must they observe *all* the details, but they must test them.

If you plan a trip with a person with long fingers and knotty joints, he will spend forever deciding what to take and why. But once packed, he will be prepared for any possible emergency. He may be slow, but he is certainly thorough.

People with long, smooth-jointed fingers think more intuitively and therefore quickly than people with long fingers and knotty joints. They are instinctively graceful. They worry about details, however, and like "finish."

THE KNOTS ON YOUR FINGERS

You can find knots on any size or shape of hand. They always mean that the person takes longer to make up his mind or change it than the average person. Long knotty fingers on a stiff, long hand should warn you that you can't make this person decide anything quickly. What's more, you'll have an even tougher time trying to persuade him to change his mind once it's made up.

On the small flexible hand with short fingers that shows fast impulsive thinking in every other way, knotty fingers might be a balancing factor, adding a needed ounce of thoughtfulness.

The "first knots"—those nearest the fingertips—are called the knots of mental order or "philosophic" knots. They indicate orderly thinking. People with such knots accept nothing until they have proved it to their own satisfaction.

The "second knots" on the lower joints of the fingers are called the "knots of material order" and indicate a pragmatic, businesslike sort of person.

Smooth fingers without knots at the joints are characteristic of quick, instinctive or intuitive thinking.

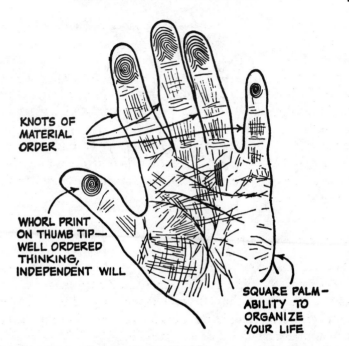

KNOTS OF
MATERIAL
ORDER

WHORL PRINT
ON THUMB TIP—
WELL ORDERED
THINKING,
INDEPENDENT WILL

SQUARE PALM—
ABILITY TO
ORGANIZE
YOUR LIFE

Knots of material order belong to the person who can organize the practical details of life. If this is an outstanding characteristic, it will be repeated in other ways.

Desbarrolles classed the combinations of knots and finger shapes as follows:

Shape	*Leanings*
Smooth fingers and pointed tips	inspiration divination
Smooth fingers and square tips	politics philosophy art based on nature practical planning

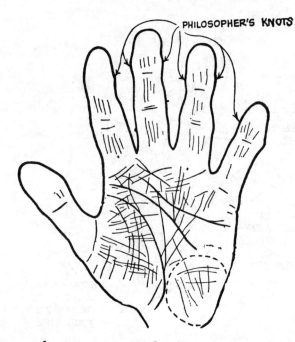

Knots on the joints nearest the fingertips, or "Philosopher's Knots," show order in ideas.

Smooth fingers and spatulate tips	great activity
	calculation
	mechanics
	administration
	art that depicts action
First knots and pointed tips	Utopianism
First knots and square tips	absolute justice
	useful work
First knots and spatulate tips	inventive realism
Second knots and pointed tips	inner struggle
	inspiration versus calculation

Shape	Leanings
Second knots and square tips	orderliness love of discipline
Second knots and spatulate tips	practical enterprise military tactics
Both knots and pointed tips	inspired inventions restlessness
Both knots and square tips	natural science history common sense
Both knots and spatulate tips	exact science physical activity the invention or running of machines exploration

Desbarrolles considered the conic tips half way between the pointed and the square. He called them versatile—a combination of the practicality of the square tips with the inspiration of the pointed tips.

THE THREE SECTIONS OF THE FINGER

The three sections of your fingers indicate the three spheres of interest for your particular talents. If your hand is long, your fingertips are probably your longest area. This section stresses your interest in ideas.

Long fingertips are characteristic of the mystic, the idealist, the intellectual or anyone who considers thought more important than action. The most sensitive and specialized nerves in the hand are located in your fingertips. The sensitive person adept at using his hands to explore and learn has the long tips. You usually see them on long

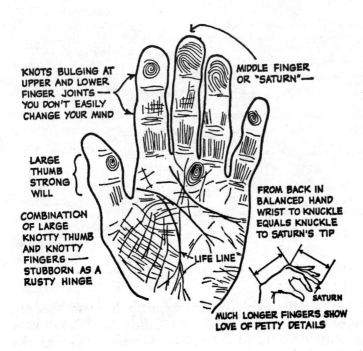

KNOTS BULGING AT UPPER AND LOWER FINGER JOINTS — YOU DON'T EASILY CHANGE YOUR MIND

MIDDLE FINGER OR "SATURN"—

LARGE THUMB STRONG WILL

COMBINATION OF LARGE KNOTTY THUMB AND KNOTTY FINGERS — STUBBORN AS A RUSTY HINGE

FROM BACK IN BALANCED HAND WRIST TO KNUCKLE EQUALS KNUCKLE TO SATURN'S TIP

LIFE LINE

SATURN

MUCH LONGER FINGERS SHOW LOVE OF PETTY DETAILS

hands, though they are found on all shapes of hands and always emphasize a strong interest in ideas. The fingertips of mental patients are often too long, showing that their own distorted ideas are more important to them than reality. However, unusually long tips are not a sign of insanity. The tip sections emphasize thought, and the sections of your fingers closest to your palm have an opposite meaning. If the lower areas are bulging and sausage-shaped in proportion to the other two sections, they emphasize sensuality, the desire for material comforts. People with fingers like this want the good things in life in large doses. If these lower sections are highly padded in the back but not large all the way around, they emphasize a love of quality. The gourmet fits into this category.

If the lowest sections are waisted, it indicates an inquiring mind and willingness to work hard. These sections are often slightly longer than the other two sections as viewed inside your hand. If they are noticeably long, out of proportion to the other sections, they indicate a very down-to-earth, materialistic nature.

The middle sections of the fingers are longest in the hands of people who emphasize practical planning. Metaphysics does not interest them as much as balanced checkbooks or the arrangement of their time to best practical advantage. If the middle sections look short in proportion to the other two sections, it's usually because the tips are long. If the middle sections are decidedly short in proportion to the other two, you know that the person is not balanced and lacks the ability to cope with life smoothly. The tip sections of the fingers are likely to be somewhat short in a broad hand. They emphasize the fact that the person prefers action to complicated brain work.

When all three spheres of interest are in balance, the three areas are in exact proportion to one another.

CHAPTER V

THE MOUNTS: KEYS
TO CHARACTER DEVELOPMENT

"Man will become better when you show him what he is like."
                                        —Anton Chekov.

The hills and valleys of the hand and groups of lines that cluster in one part of the hand but leave another as smooth as silk show reservoirs of power or desire, or the combination of the two that may lead to fulfillment.

"Mounts," or special areas of the hand, are related to different facets of your character. They show what kind of instinctive energy you have and how you use it.

In some hands, each separate area has its own cushion of flesh. Therefore, these areas are called "mounts" even though they are flat as a pane of glass. Don't be confused by the traditional use of the word "mount." Here the name refers to the area, not to padding or elevation. A mount can be concave or sunken.

Look at Desbarrolles' picture of the mounts and you will see the kind of action depicted by each mount. On the elevation at the base of the thumb, you will see a boy and girl holding hands. This area of the hand is called the

Desbarrolles, an artist as well as a hand-reader, used this picture of mount meanings for his "Revélations Complètes." (Photograph courtesy of The Library of Congress.)

Mount of Venus, and it indicates warmth, vitality and sensuality.

On the outside heel of the hand, Desbarrolles has pictured a sailing ship. This mount is named Luna, or Moon, and is the index of imagination, mysticism and restlessness, hence love of the sea.

The battleground shown in the center of the palm is the Plain of Mars. If it is sunken like a bowl, and all the other mounts are low, you lack the spirit to struggle against adversity.

The part of the battlefield on the outside edge of the hand, and the determined-looking thinker standing on the line above the warriors are both on the Mount of Mars—the seat of endurance.

Under the index finger, in Desbarrolles' picture, is the Mount of Jupiter, where we read ambition and leadership marked by a picture of a king on his throne.

The picture of a miner under the long middle finger, on the Mount of Saturn, indicates the love of such basic and down-to-earth pursuits as mining, characteristic of the serious-minded, sober people with this mount large or heavily marked.

The muse plucking at her lyre under the ring finger tells us this mount shows flair and style, so necessary to the artist. It is the Mount of Apollo.

The Mount of Mercury under the little finger indicates the astuteness and fluency so necessary to the orator, and so Desbarrolles has pictured an orator there.

Modern hand-readers place aggressiveness in an active Mount of Mars at the base of the thumb just above the Mount of Venus.

(Other pictures on Desbarrolles' hand have nothing to do with the mounts. On the life-line, circling the Mount of Venus, we see the life span from the cradle to the grave.

On the thumb, we see Will paying no attention to Reason.)

Using a hand-print, mark with dotted lines any areas on your hand that have fleshy padding on them. Label each area: high, medium or low. This padding, if firm, shows physical energy. The amount of padding indicates the amount of energy expended in the direction of any given mount. For example, if the padding under the index finger

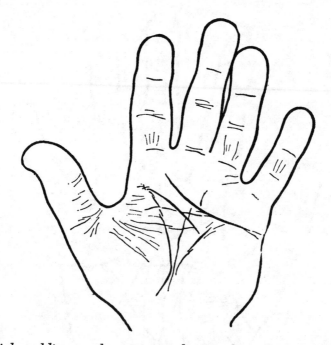

High padding on the mounts indicates physical energy.

is high and firm, you are actively energetic in your efforts to be a leader. You would lead a parade just as readily as you would write a letter to your senator. If you ran for senator yourself, you would be apt to direct your own very active campaign. The area of the hand where the high padding is shows how you use your energy.

If the padding is medium-soft, it indicates straightforward mental energy—the kind often found in people who are mentally alert but don't get much physical exercise. An intellectual leader would have this sort of padding on the Mount of Ambition. But flabby padding on the Mount of Ambition indicates love of luxury.

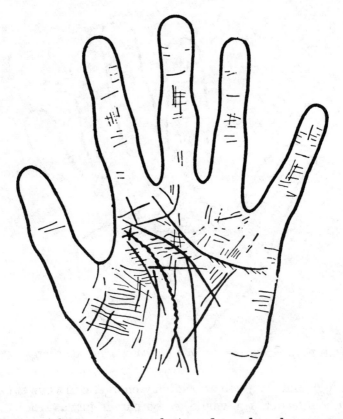

Groups of lines on mounts that are flat or low show nervous energy.

A flat or nearly flat mount covered with concentrations of lines is a sign of nervous energy. One clear, deep line or a balanced and well delineated group of lines mean that this nervous energy is being used to good effect.

Scrambled and faltering lines on a mount warn us that we've been using the quality of the mount in the wrong way. Often such lines reveal a part of our nature that has gotten temporarily out of control. For example, on the Mount of Ambition scrambled lines would show destructive pride. Remember, however, that markings change.

Vertical lines on a mount (they run in the same direction as the fingers) are a good sign unless there are more than three or four. But horizontal lines suggest obstacles.

If your hand is covered by a network of fine lines with the main lines clearly marked, you'll have to be a bit careful how you read them. The fine lines tell you that you are somewhat impressionable and high-strung, but don't interpret them to mean that you have scrambled lines on every mount. The strongest reading of such hands should be given to the most clearly marked lines.

A high mount covered with lines shows complex and passionate feelings and hence lack of control. On the Mount of active Mars, for example, it would indicate too much aggressiveness.

Patterns formed on a mount by papillary ridges of the skin reveal a great deal as to how you use the abilities indicated by that mount. Each of the mounts on your hand at the base of your fingers has a skin-ridge pattern called the apex of the mount. The natural place for this apex is directly under the center of the finger and approximately in the center of the mount. However, the apex under the little finger is apt to be closer to the inside edge of that finger.

When they are in their normal places, these apexes indi-

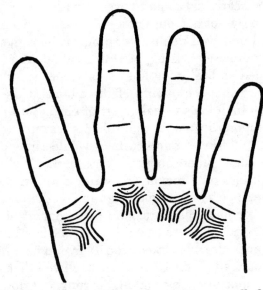

Usual position for the skin-ridge patterns called "apexes" found on the finger mounts.

cate a balanced use of the ability shown by the mount. If they are out of place they add to the significance of the mount toward which they lean.

Sometimes you will find other patterns in the papillary ridges of the skin, often in the shape of tiny whorls or bull's eyes. These may be on any mount in the hand. We'll see later how they add importance to the mount.

The mounts, then, show what kind of energy or drive we have and the general way in which we use it. You read the mounts under your fingers along with the finger. The mount indicates how much energy you have, your finger shows more precisely how you use that energy.

Most mounts are associated with one of the lines of your hand. This line usually has the same name as the mount and is related to it in meaning.

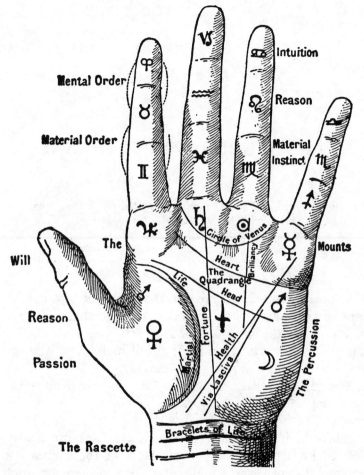

Principal lines are Life, Heart, Head and Fate (here called "Fortune"). Astrological signs on this old picture show the planets believed to be related to parts of the hand in the days when palmistry was combined with astrology.

CHAPTER VI

THE LINES OF YOUR HAND

"Chiromancie—old as the world, perfected by famous men and the most sublime geniuses—is so simple that a child can learn it in several days."

—Adolphe Desbarrolles.

The lines in your hand are like the words of a song—the tune of the song sets the mood just as the shape of your hands shows the general trend of your personality. The lines, like the lyrics of the song, tell more exactly what you are, where you're headed and why.

The general formation of the lines in your hand is far more important than the location of any one line or any special sign in the hand.

A broad hand is inclined to have fewer and more clearly defined lines than a long hand. More of these lines are horizontal than vertical in direction. When there are a lot of lines on a broad hand and many of them run up and down, the person possesses much of the sensitivity usually associated with long hands. Poets usually have broad hands with many lines.

A long hand usually has many more lines (also more vertical lines) than a broad hand. Also, there are generally more "faults"—breaks, chained formation, islands on the lines or wavering lines. In a long hand where the main lines are clearly defined, a few "faults" aren't serious, though they do indicate some inner struggle. A large number of "faults" suggests that the person is oversensitive, inhibited, nervous and unable to do all the things he wants to do.

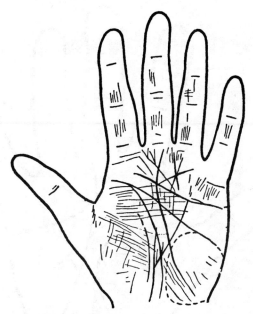

Here's the hand of someone who doesn't let her worries overwhelm her. There are many fine lines, but the main lines are clearly marked.

In general, women's hands have more lines than men's. The man with many lines in his hand is a "thinking" man rather than a man of action.

If you have a long hand with few but clearly marked lines, you are almost as much a person of direct action as your broad-handed neighbor.

You will notice in the "Table of Line Meanings" that few lines and average skin show more physical than nervous energy. This doesn't necessarily mean a lack of nervous energy, but does mean that if nervous energy exists **it** is translated directly into action.

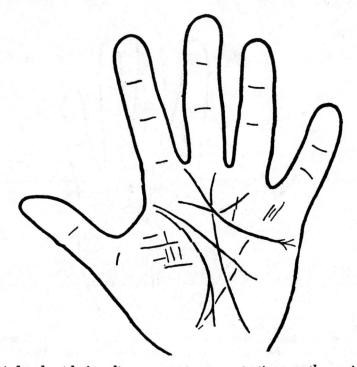

A hand with few lines suggests concentration on the main issues.

Each line in the hand is related to the mount where it begins and ends. The two mounts and the clarity of the line determine its meanings. Therefore I will explain the mounts and lines together in the chapters which follow.

Incidentally, to be considered well-marked the lines

TABLE OF LINE MEANINGS

Fine lines	Subtle perceptions
Deep lines	Strong feelings, pronounced likes and dislikes
Few lines and average or coarse skin	More physical than nervous energy
Few clearly marked lines and very fine, delicate skin	Intuitive or intellectual energy consistently directed
Many lines	Nervous energy
Many lines, main lines well marked, others superficially marked	Nervous energy, constructively channeled
Main lines not much deeper or better marked than spider web of fine lines which cover the hand	High strung and impressionable person
Lines as above with very delicate fine-grained skin	Very sensitive person—you need calm
Main lines and many other lines all deeply marked	Deep feelings plus some inner conflicts
Lines as above plus high mounts	Passionate feelings
Lines as above plus flat or hollow mounts	Strong desires, more intellectual than emotional
Main lines badly marked with breaks, islands, chained formations	Nervous or physical strain, tendency toward hysteria when under pressure
Accessory lines wavering like wriggling snakes or forming scrambled, tangled groups	Nervous over-stimulation or rundown physical condition
Lines broad and marked like a trench in coarse skin	Undeveloped intelligence
Dead pale lines	Lack of energy
Yellow lines	Nervousness and inhibitions
Red lines	Strong feelings
Pink lines (if well-marked)	Healthy body and mind

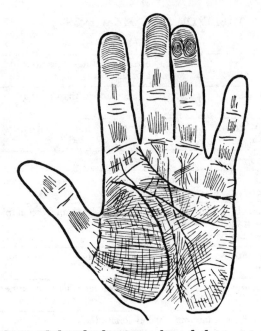

Fine skin with hundreds of tiny lines belongs to a person too sensitive for his own comfort.

must be clearly marked without breaks, islands or chains. The lines of life, head and heart must be present and fairly long, and if there are more than a few lines on the hand, the line of fate must be present, too. (You find an exception to this in the hands of people who are brilliant but entirely unconventional. They may lack the fate-line.) Your hands are not likely to be perfectly marked unless you are either perfect or very simple. To be really badly marked, the lines must be tangled or broken in several places, and they must have an uncertain, wavering look.

To evaluate the exact combination of line type and hand shape, see the table "How to Combine Hand Shapes and Line Meanings."

GOT SOMETHING TO SAY ?
— CARL SANDBURG

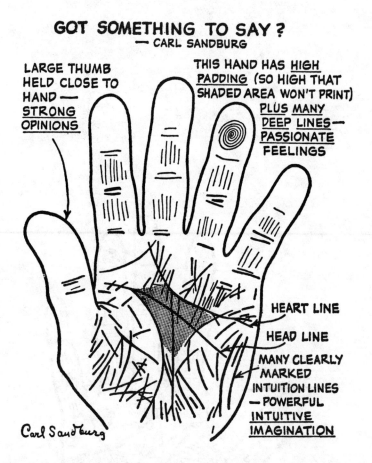

LARGE THUMB HELD CLOSE TO HAND — STRONG OPINIONS

THIS HAND HAS HIGH PADDING (SO HIGH THAT SHADED AREA WON'T PRINT) PLUS MANY DEEP LINES — PASSIONATE FEELINGS

HEART LINE

HEAD LINE

MANY CLEARLY MARKED INTUITION LINES — POWERFUL INTUITIVE IMAGINATION

Carl Sandburg

Many lines deeply marked, plus high mounts, show emotions so deep they must be expressed. This can be an advantage to a creative person.

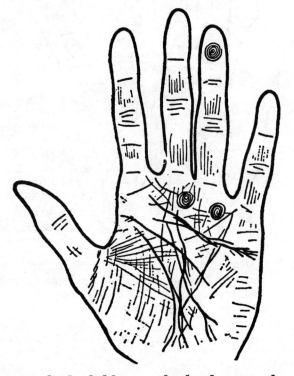

Many twisted, islanded lines in this hand suggest the owner's hardest struggles are within herself.

HOW TO COMBINE HAND SHAPES AND
LINE MEANINGS

LINES	BROAD AND MEDIUM HAND	NARROW HAND
Few lines deep and well-marked	You are outgoing, purposeful, with clear, simple goals.	You are poised with clear personal goal
Lines few, deep and falteringly marked (especially with coarse skin)	You are energetic but not sure where you're going. When upset, like a bull in a china shop, or very depressed.	You are not sure of yourself — therefore, easily hurt—but may still have a clear over-all sense of direction.
Lines few, fine, and well-marked	Subtle perceptions and a clear goal.	You are subtle, sensitive and know how to get what you want.
Lines few, fine, and badly-marked	Slightly chained, islanded or feathery lines may show delicately tuned nerves. If the lines are *very* badly marked—delicate nerves and superficial emotions or hysteria.	If the lines are chained or feathery — delicate nerves and the need to be alone or quiet often. Very badly-marked lines —selfishness
Main lines deep and fairly well-marked, many other lines superficial	You are outgoing and purposeful enough to make your sensitivity to others an asset. With high mounts—very emotional. Example: Ernestine Schumann-Heink	You are intuitive, highly strung but can make this an asset (especially with a normal or large thumb) Example: Mary Martin
Main lines and spiderweb of fine lines, all equally superficial	You are impressionable and high strung, but if the hand is firm, energetic. If flabby, a dreamer.	You are so high strung that you need harmonious surroundings to keep on an even keel.
Many lines—all deeply marked	Deep feelings usually find an outlet. This is often the expressive hand of a writer or musician. Example: Maurice Ravel	Intense feelings. This is often the hand of the philosopher.
Many lines deeply and falteringly marked with many faults	Strong inner conflicts, possibly with the energy to manage anyway	Deep feelings but strong inhibitions. Tormented emotions.

CHAPTER VII

"GOOD" AND "BAD" HANDS

"It is easier to know water ten fathoms deep than a man one fathom tall."
                                        —Old Korean proverb.

Judging by their letters to me, readers of my newspaper feature, *Helping Hands*, seemed to have two chief questions in mind: "Am I good or bad?" and "Am I lucky or unlucky?"

In general, the shape of your hand indicates your approach to life while your mounts show the kind of energy you have and how you use it.

Your lines reflect your own awareness of what you are and where you are headed. Therefore, your lines can change. The mannerisms of your hands, the way in which you hold them, their color and temperature provide clues to the state of your feelings.

Above all, you want to know: "What is there about my hand that shows chances for happiness and success?"

Happiness is most easily discovered by the person with a balanced hand in which no one mount is greatly out of proportion to the rest, the lines are clearly marked and medium in number, the fingers are straight and evenly set and the hand is neither remarkably flexible nor stiff.

If the vertical lines are also long and clearly marked, you can assume that the person is well balanced, sensitive and possessed of good sense of purpose. Such a hand is very rare, however. Most of us can get a great deal out of life with less balanced and clearly marked hands.

We often find genius in the very unbalanced hand. The owner of the unbalanced hand may be successful under the right circumstances.

The so-called "bad" hand shows us at a glance that this person has had a hard time getting along with himself. Almost all of us have at least one bad characteristic in our hands.

If you would imagine a hand with all the signs of a warped personality, you would find twisted fingers unevenly placed; scrambled and twisted lines with many breaks and islands; hollow mounts or one mount developed out of all proportion to the others; chalk white, alarmingly red or vividly yellow coloring; a hand tightly clenched or flabbily open like wilted lettuce; a very large or very small thumb out of proportion to the rest of the hand, especially the fingers.

Luckily, you probably won't be shaking hands with anybody like this, but you will come across hands with one or more of these faults. Any one of these qualities is the hallmark of a person who has trouble solving his problems, and two of them indicates that he is in even greater trouble.

For example, a small thumb is the sign of a person who lacks the will power to overcome natural faults. When the small thumb is combined with flabby or hollow hands, this person is not only unable to conquer his faults but feels that his faults have conquered him.

Old palmistry books, written before man knew as much as he does today about how to cure his mental and physical ills, were inclined to associate depressing predictions with problem hands. All of us have heard for example, that a short life-line is the sign of early death. As we shall see, this sign is not nearly as gloomy as tradition would have us think.

As you read hands, notice how they reflect the serious problems people have. But if your hand reflects your problems, it may also show those positive traits you need to solve them.

CHAPTER VIII

LIFE, LOVE AND WILL POWER

"Man is the only animal that blushes, or needs to."
—Mark Twain.

Don't bother pulling petals off a daisy to find out if your true love loves you—just look at her Mount of Venus. This mount shows instinctive warmth and vitality.

If your Mount of Venus is high and the line of life encircling it loops far out into the palm, you are most likely warm-hearted and vibrantly alive. This mount is associated with love—the instinctive, overflowing kind of love a person feels who has an excess of vitality.

The high mount also goes with a love for all the good things of life. The person with this mount is sensual as well as emotional. When we are overflowing with warmth, we sing, therefore it's not surprising that the high mount is associated with a love of melody.

When your Mount of Venus is a thin, low pad and the life-line runs close to the thumb, you are not sensual by nature and your love for your fellow beings is mental rather than physical. You are content to share their interests.

If the Mount of Venus is large and soft, it indicates an exaggerated love of pleasure. If it is large, soft and pink, it is a sign of cheerfulness and the desire to share cher-

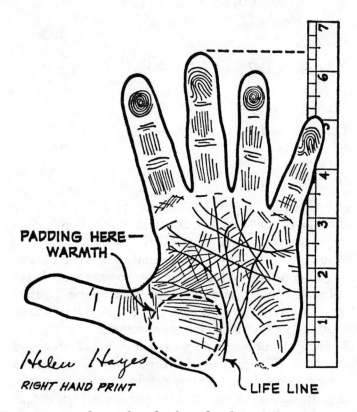

PADDING HERE—
WARMTH

Helen Hayes
RIGHT HAND PRINT   LIFE LINE

You are warm-hearted and vibrantly alive if your Mount of Venus is high and wide.

ished luxuries. If it is large and flabby and dead-white, you are selfishly sensual.

If your mount is thick and hard and there are two mounts of Mars that are also thick and full, your vitality reveals another side entirely. You may be warm-hearted, but you are extremely combative. No one should get into

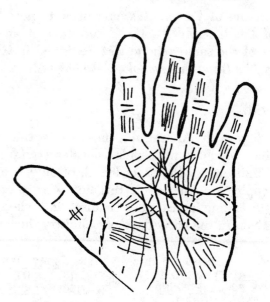

*If your Mount of Venus is thin and low, love for you is more
mental than physical.*

a fight with you unless they have as much push as you do—
and that's a lot.

A grill of lines on the Mount of Venus shows a need for
affection. On a high, full mount, a deeply marked grill is
the sign of a passionate nature.

From time to time, the study of palmistry has been combined with the study of astrology, and a certain type of
hand was supposed to show the influence of the planet
Venus. This hand had (as you might expect) a large full
Mount of Venus, but in addition it was generally small,
plump, and dimpled. It was soft but not flabby and had
short, smooth fingers and a short, flexible thumb.

You can see how such a hand would emphasize all of
the spontaneous warmth and love of luxury associated

with a full Mount of Venus. (It's interesting to note that this type of hand nearly fits the description of an endocrine type of the same general sort described in Charlotte Wolff's *The Hand in Psychological Diagnosis*, p. 22.)

THE LIFE-LINE

The boundary of the Mount of Venus nearest the palm is the life-line, which many people consider (quite mistakenly) an indicator of the exact length of one's life. At one time people thought that if this line were short in both hands, its ending indicated the natural time when you would die. Even in the early days of palmistry, however,

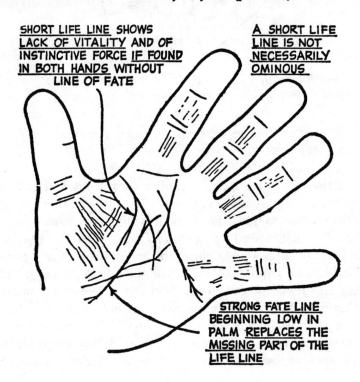

SHORT LIFE LINE SHOWS LACK OF VITALITY AND OF INSTINCTIVE FORCE IF FOUND IN BOTH HANDS WITHOUT LINE OF FATE

A SHORT LIFE LINE IS NOT NECESSARILY OMINOUS

STRONG FATE LINE BEGINNING LOW IN PALM REPLACES THE MISSING PART OF THE LIFE LINE people believed that with a strong will (shown by a large thumb) or great attention to health, you could outlive your natural span of years.

Today, life insurance tables show that most of us outlive what the nineteenth century considered our natural span of years. Many people reading this book have had their lives saved by modern medical techniques and drugs. And many of us, without realizing it, have extended our life span through improved public sanitation.

Still, the life-line shows a lot about ourselves. For example, the man with a short life-line would do better to live by his wits than his brawn. And a life-line that appears short may actually be lengthened by a strong fate-line on the lower part of the hand.

Palmists often read the timing of events on the life-line. But while some palmists date our childhood years from that part of the line that lies under the index finger, others begin down near the wrist. Both seem to obtain fairly good results—a sure sign that dating events along the life-line is really a matter of intuition rather than science. You'll read more about this dating system in a later chapter.

Regardless of which end of the life-line represents childhood, it's interesting to note that all systems of dating assign the age of thirty-five to the same approximate spot— the center of the line as it runs from the edge of the hand under the index finger all the way down to the wrist. Islands or breaks in the line are supposed to show periods of physical or nervous stress (the age depends, of course, on whether you're reading up or down the line).

The life-line tells us a good deal about our temperament and vitality. We don't need to follow a system of dating to learn that a line with many breaks or islands

HARRY GOLDEN

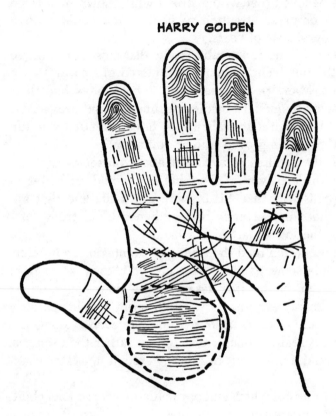

When the life-line sends a branch toward the index finger, it shows ambition.

belongs to a person who needs to take care of himself and get plenty of relaxation.

If your life-line curves far out into your hand, you are a person of action. Even if the Mount of Venus is fairly flat, a far curving life-line is the sign of a physically vigorous person. On the other hand, a life-line that curves closely around the thumb indicates you prefer mental rather than physical activity.

Under the index finger, the life-line may be attached and close to the head-line above it: this is a sign of great caution. Again, the two lines may be widely separated at the start—a sign of rash independence and impulsiveness— or the lines may be only slightly separated, which indicates a more moderate form of independence.

If your life- and head-lines touch at the point of origin, you have a balanced nature. If your lines are joined for as much as a third the length of your head-line, you are timid. This is particularly true in a conic hand. In a square hand, it is a sign of caution.

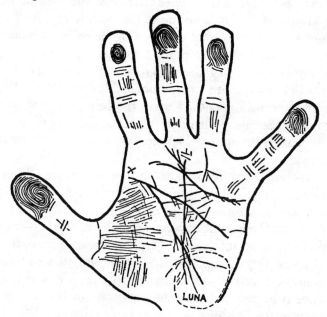

When the life-line ends out in the hand near the Mount of Luna, it indicates restlessness.

If your life-line displays a branch extending to the top of the Mount of Jupiter (the mount under the index finger), you will probably attain success through your abilities and determination.

If your life-line near the wrist curves around the Mount of Venus toward the outside of the hand, you probably have deep love of home—like the Texan who keeps a little urn of Texas soil on his mantelpiece when he's far from the Lone Star State.

On the other hand, if your life-line is almost a diagonal line across your hand that passes quite close to the Mount of the Moon, you are extremely restless and probably have a strong desire to travel.

You have worries if all lines that cross the life-line from the Mount of Venus continue to the middle of your hand. When you have a great number of these lines, you are someone who worries so much that you sap your strength and impede much of the progress you might make.

Traditionally, these worry lines are supposed to indicate specific worries depending upon the line or mount where they end. People with many of these lines need an important interest upon which to concentrate their mental energy.

Branches rising from the life-line are called "lines of personal effort." The person with such lines is making a strong bid to improve his life.

Lines on the Mount of Venus parallel to the life-line are called "lines of influence." Hindu palmists in particular emphasize these lines. Each is supposed to represent a person who exercises an influence on your life, and the influence is in proportion to the proximity of the line of influence to the life-line.

This system appears to work, though perhaps only because people with many lines on the Mount of Venus need affection and are influenced by many people around them.

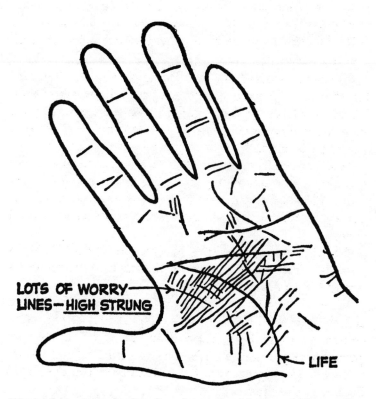

Lines that cross the life-line from the Mount of Venus show worries.

A line running beside the life-line and inside of it on the Mount of Venus (which is almost as clearly marked as the life-line) is called the Line of Mars. It is not a line of influence, and in general it appears to show more power of resistance in a hand with a badly marked life-line and tremendous vitality in a hand with a stronger life-line. We'll learn more about this line in a later chapter.

CHAPTER IX

ALL THUMBS

"The gentle Norman barons would seem to have been im-
pressed with the importance of (the thumb) when they
hung up their enemies thereby."
                                        —Stanislas d'Arpentigny.

The thumb shows more about you at a glance than any
other part of the hand. While the Mount of Venus shows
whether you are warm and fiery or cool and collected, and
the life-line shows physical vitality and resistance, the
thumb shows whether you can deliberately make the best
of all your talents and abilities or whether your success
will depend on chance.

The average thumb reaches half way up the lowest section of the index finger.

A large thumb belongs to a person who works out a plan
and, as far as his other abilities allow, either sticks to the
plan or changes it after careful consideration—the way a
map-maker might change a map if he discovered a mistake
in it. A large thumb is said, therefore, to go with a strong
will.

The person with a small thumb is ruled by instinct and
emotion. On a short-term basis, such a person may seem
more willful than someone with a long thumb since he is

more influenced by the whim of the moment than by any long-range plan. He has less self-control than the long-thumbed person and a weaker will. This person depends on chance and the help of other people. With talent and intelligence, this person can be extremely successful, but he will succeed by fits and starts of inspiration rather than by any single-minded drive.

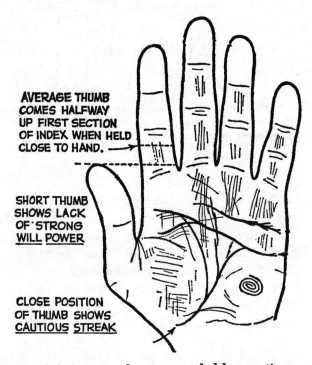

AVERAGE THUMB COMES HALFWAY UP FIRST SECTION OF INDEX WHEN HELD CLOSE TO HAND. ➤

SHORT THUMB SHOWS LACK OF STRONG WILL POWER

CLOSE POSITION OF THUMB SHOWS CAUTIOUS STREAK

Small thumb belongs to the person ruled by emotion.

Women are inclined to have shorter thumbs than men, and most of the old jokes about women are aimed at the short-thumbed variety. For example, there's the old story about women in business: if you treat them like women, they get the better of you, and if you treat them like men, they cry.

The shape of the thumb and length of each section is important. Here's what it shows about you:

A long, broad tip section and short palm section are the

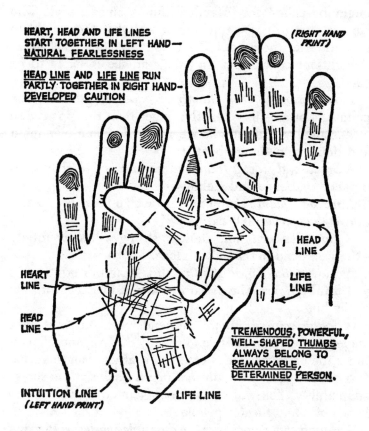

HEART, HEAD AND LIFE LINES START TOGETHER IN LEFT HAND— NATURAL FEARLESSNESS

HEAD LINE AND LIFE LINE RUN PARTLY TOGETHER IN RIGHT HAND— DEVELOPED CAUTION

(RIGHT HAND PRINT)

HEART LINE

HEAD LINE

HEAD LINE

LIFE LINE

TREMENDOUS, POWERFUL, WELL-SHAPED THUMBS ALWAYS BELONG TO REMARKABLE, DETERMINED PERSON.

INTUITION LINE (LEFT HAND PRINT)

LIFE LINE

Large thumb usually belongs to a person who goes by a plan and has strong will power. Sir Edmund Hillary's hands show will, plus caution and courage, that helped him conquer Mt. Everest.

signs of a steamroller will. If the tip section is slightly longer, look for some stubborness. If the tip section is much longer, you leap before you look and can't be reasoned with.

A long palm section and short tip section mean that you're better at giving advice than acting decisively. This might be called the "Hamlet" thumb since people who have it tend to go on thinking about what they ought to do until after they should have done it. They reach well-thought-out conclusions and their advice is likely to be good.

Two sections of the thumb of equal length with the palm section possibly slightly longer than the tip section means good equilibrium between knowing your own mind and doing something about it.

A broad and stocky thumb of normal length shows endurance, patience and stability.

A waisted palm section means tact (unless the tip section is overpoweringly larger).

A long, slender thumb shows a strong will and subtlety —the iron hand in the velvet glove.

A marble-like tip on the thumb is a sign of erratic will and fitful temper. This feature is also associated with fits of the blues.

A double-jointed thumb that bends back almost at right angles shows adaptability and usually extravagance. Sometimes the extravagance is emotional rather than financial.

A double-jointed thumb that bends back slightly shows adaptability. You will see a double-jointed thumb on the hands of many theater people.

A thumb that's both short and double-jointed is the sign of an impressionable person.

A pointed thumb means that you're quick and impulsive.

A conic thumb indicates less will than a square thumb,

but more than a pointed one. If it is very long, it is a sign of will and tact.

A *square thumb* indicates common sense.

A *spatulate thumb* is a sign of impatience.

A *flat, broad thumb* shaped like a canoe paddle shows a strong will backed by nervous energy rather than physical strength. Sculptors and potters often have a thumb like this with a little bump of flesh showing a concentration of nerve endings on the palm side of the tip section.

*   *   *

By combining what you know about the thumb and the Mount of Venus, here's how you might answer the question so often put to hand-readers, "Will I marry and live happily ever after?"

—High or medium Mount of Venus and normal or slightly large thumb—probably.

—High or medium Mount of Venus and huge thumb—marry somebody who wants a boss.

—High or medium Venus and small thumb—be careful or you will marry in haste and repent at leisure.

—Flat, grilled Venus and large thumb—you need affection and have the perseverance to find it.

—Flat, grilled Venus and small thumb—marry the person with a high Venus and large thumb. You need love and a boss too.

—Low Venus with life-line running close to the large thumb—you'll marry because of mutual interests.

—Low, small Venus and small thumb—you'll marry for security or will be perfectly happy unmarried.

*   *   *

The position of your thumb is also important. Several positions have already been mentioned, but check with your hand prints to see how you normally hold your hand.

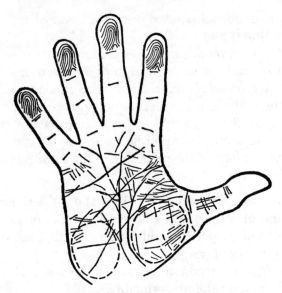

*Thumbs held at right angles to the hands show an open mind;
in a bad hand, lack of self-discipline.*

A thumb held very wide, almost at right angles to the
hand, shows an extremely open mind. Hindu palmistry
says that the thumb opened at a 90° angle from the hand
is the sign of a balanced soul.

The normal angle between the thumb and hand is from
about 45° to 60°—a medium position. Self-reliant people
usually have this angle.

If you hold your thumb any closer to your hand, you
are a cautious person, usually set in his ways and sometimes secretive.

If your thumb is bent as though it were stooping to look
shorter, you are probably tense and lack self-confidence
to such an extent that you are sometimes anti-social and
hard to deal with. Like the turned-in thumb, this may
reflect a temporary state of mind.

A slightly turned-in thumb combined with the long, little finger that shows cleverness may belong to a person who manages to compensate for any lack of confidence. A successful business woman I know with a hand like this does "dry runs" before every important appointment in that part of her city that's not familiar to her. She makes a trip during her lunch hour to the new address to be sure

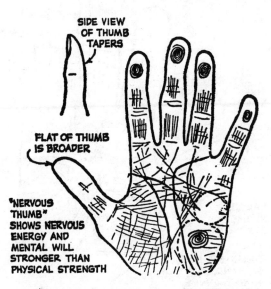

SIDE VIEW OF THUMB TAPERS

FLAT OF THUMB IS BROADER

"NERVOUS THUMB" SHOWS NERVOUS ENERGY AND MENTAL WILL STRONGER THAN PHYSICAL STRENGTH

Held at a medium angle (45°-60°) to the hand, the thumb suggests self-reliance.

she knows how to get there and how long it will take. Then she can arrive for the business appointment relaxed and on time.

Sometimes you'll see a hand print in which a thumb of normal length seems to be straining upward together with the index finger. The owner of this hand is making a tremendous effort to carry out his plans. He is tense because he senses that he is pushing himself beyond his strength.

The "best" thumb for any hand is the one that's in proportion to the rest of the hand.

A broad, firm, bulging hand with only an average thumb still shows plenty of drive.

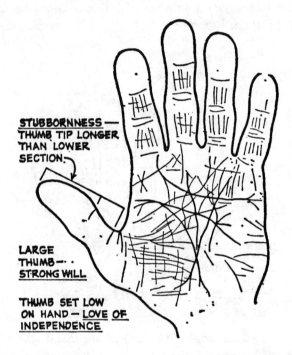

STUBBORNNESS —
THUMB TIP LONGER
THAN LOWER
SECTION.

LARGE
THUMB — .
STRONG WILL

THUMB SET LOW
ON HAND — LOVE OF
INDEPENDENCE

A slender, sensitive-looking hand needs a slightly longer thumb—almost (but not quite) to the first knuckle of the index finger—if the person is to have the push and perseverance to turn his dreams into realities.

The extremely mobile thumb—one that offers no resistance when you bend it this way and that—shows inner flexibility and often extravagance.

The very stiff thumb, which can hardly be bent out of

its natural position, belongs to a dogmatic person. Don't waste your breath trying to make him change his mind.

Of course, a large thumb is not a talisman that insures perseverance. In a clumsy hand with tortuous-looking lines or almost no lines, this thumb shows a potentiality that for some reason you can't use.

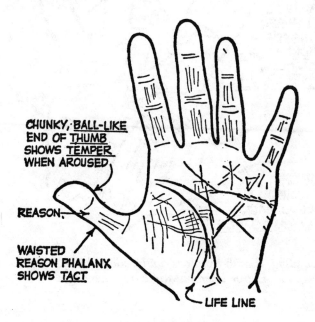

CHUNKY, BALL-LIKE END OF THUMB SHOWS TEMPER WHEN AROUSED

REASON

WAISTED REASON PHALANX SHOWS TACT

LIFE LINE

The small thumb sometimes belongs to people who spend their lives helping others.

A person whose abilities must be consciously controlled —anyone whose work requires stick-to-itiveness—needs a thumb of normal or large size in order to succeed.

Those whose gifts are a welling-up from the subconscious may be successful by force of their talents without long thumbs—hence, the short thumb is sometimes found on the successful artist, wife, or missionary.

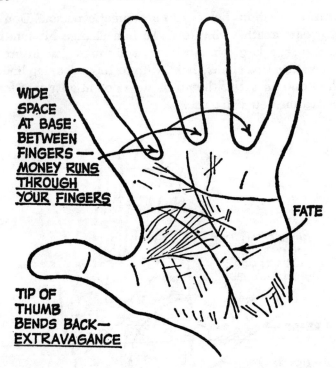

WIDE
SPACE
AT BASE
BETWEEN
FINGERS —
MONEY RUNS
THROUGH
YOUR FINGERS

FATE

TIP OF
THUMB
BENDS BACK—
EXTRAVAGANCE

Back-bending thumb-tip goes with adaptability as well as extravagance. Latter is emphasized by other signs.

CHAPTER X

"PUSH"
AND THE BRAINS TO USE IT

"He who enjoys doing and enjoys what he has done is happy."

—Goethe.

The Mount of Active Mars (often called Lower Mars because it is below the head-line) is often treated as part of the Mount of Venus. It is located at the base of the thumb but above the Mount of Venus.

Both mounts together—Venus and Mars—indicate emotional warmth. But when the Mount of Mars is firm and bulges, this warmth takes the form of energy, push and combativeness. A true fighter will have bulges on both this combative Mount of Mars and the Mount of Passive Mars (on the other side of the hand).

The line of Mars, which starts on the Mount of Active Mars, looks like a double life-line. If the mount is high, this line indicates even greater physical resistance and a tendency to fight for what you want. Tradition has it that this line spells success in love for women and success in war for men. President Eisenhower has the line of Mars.

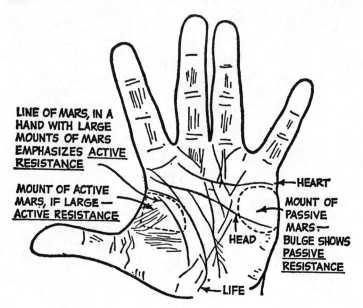

Active Mars shows constructive energy as well as active resistance.

THE HEAD-LINE

In a practical hand, the head-line will run across the hand, touching the life-line at the top boundary of the Mount of Active Mars. Then it will cross the plain of Mars and touch the lower part of the Mount of Passive Mars directly across the hand. One of the reasons why this line runs fairly straight is because the practical or useful hand is more flexible horizontally than vertically.

Basically there are two types of head-lines: the one that barely slopes and the other that slopes quite a bit. The former slopes only slightly and crosses from active to passive Mars. It is often found on a broad, practical hand, and even in a long, slender, sensitive hand it shows a streak of practicality. The go-getter has high Mounts of Mars with this line. If your Mounts of Mars are low and your thumbs large, you are less aggressive and more thoughtful but still a person of action.

The second type of head-line slopes, sometimes drastically. It may run almost all the way down to the wrist. This sort of line is likely to be found in a long, slender hand, partly because a sensitive hand is likely to be vertically flexible with many more up-and-down or sloping lines.

Even in a broad, practical hand this sort of head-line

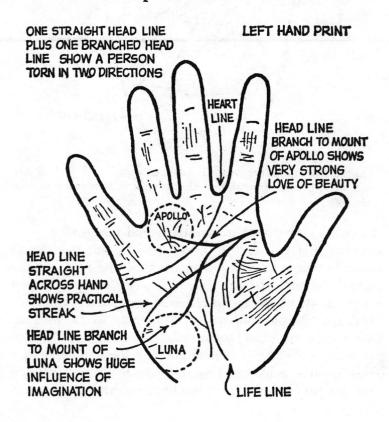

ONE STRAIGHT HEAD LINE PLUS ONE BRANCHED HEAD LINE SHOW A PERSON TORN IN TWO DIRECTIONS

LEFT HAND PRINT

HEART LINE

HEAD LINE BRANCH TO MOUNT OF APOLLO SHOWS VERY STRONG LOVE OF BEAUTY

APOLLO

HEAD LINE STRAIGHT ACROSS HAND SHOWS PRACTICAL STREAK

HEAD LINE BRANCH TO MOUNT OF LUNA SHOWS HUGE INFLUENCE OF IMAGINATION

LUNA

LIFE LINE

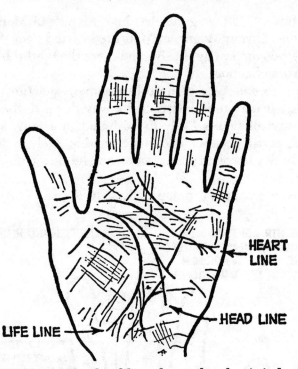

The very imaginative head-line slopes sharply. A fork at the end of any head-line shows ability to see two sides of any situation.

reveals a strong note of sensitivity and imagination. This sloping line crosses the plain of Mars, but in extreme cases it will not touch either mount. In its most sloping form, it is often found in hands that lack any padding on the Mounts of Mars—indicative of the person who finds it difficult to push ahead or do anything useful with his ideas, however good they may be.

When you see this sloping line in a forceful hand with developed Mounts of Mars and a large thumb, you can assume that the person is likely to be both imaginative and productive. Instead of day-dreaming, he writes novels or poems. If he thinks up an invention, he'll try it out.

Aside from its general direction, the line may be either very straight or somewhat curved. A slight curve goes with a more flexible mind. A head-line straight as a ram-rod suggests a calculating person.

You may have heard that the length of this line indicates your intelligence. It would be nice if it were that simple. The head-line tells you many things about your thinking, but it won't reveal your I.Q. You must study your whole hand to find that answer. Then you can draw only a very general conclusion. If the shape and markings of your

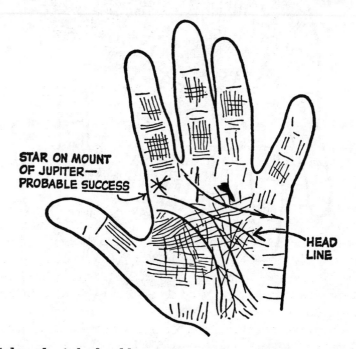

STAR ON MOUNT OF JUPITER— PROBABLE SUCCESS

HEAD LINE

A branch of the head-line to Jupiter shows ambition. With a star at the end, it shows probable success.

hand have a look of style and vitality, you are doubtless quite intelligent. The head-line in such a hand is usually long. But in the hands of idiots it can be long.

What is the meaning of the different starting places for the head-line?

When it begins on the Mount of Jupiter and curves back near the life-line—ambition and a balance between independence and caution (a good sign for an actor or politician).

With a branch to Jupiter—ambition.

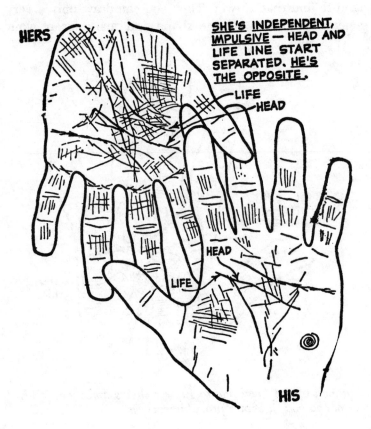

HERS

SHE'S INDEPENDENT, IMPULSIVE — HEAD AND LIFE LINE START SEPARATED. HE'S THE OPPOSITE.

LIFE
HEAD

HEAD

LIFE

HIS

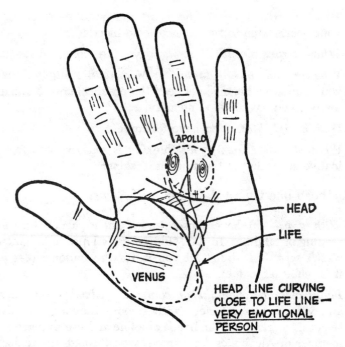

Slightly separated from the life-line—independence of thought, slight impulsiveness.

Widely separated from the life-line—impulsiveness to the point of rashness.

Curving across the life-line down into the Mount of Mars or with a strong branch curving down—perseverance in fighting your own shortcomings, sometimes a tendency to quarrel.

The signs connected with the progress of the head-line can be summarized as follows:

When it runs up into a mount or curves up toward a mount —that mount exercises an overwhelming influence on your mind.

When it runs up into the heart-line—your head controls your heart, often to the point of cold-bloodedness.

When it runs absolutely straight—you are cold and logical.

When it ends on the Mount of Mars with a slight slope—you maintain a balance between the practical and the imaginative; you have a good memory.

With a high Mars—you have fortitude.

When it slopes down—your thinking is sensitive and imaginative according to the amount of slope.

The head-line is best described as follows:

With gaps—you have lapses in judgment, hence the old reading of fatalities. In the Middle Ages a lapse in judgment wasn't safe. If it didn't let you in for the bubonic plague, it touched off a duel.

Badly marked, chainlike or containing islands—you worry and your nerves interfere with smooth thinking. (I have seen this marking on the hands of a fine and useful person, a member of Alcoholics Anonymous who through the realization of his own shortcomings and the desire to help others leads a satisfying life).

Wavering—you are pulled this way and that by desires and feelings. The quality of the mount under which the line bulges shows too much influence on your life; the quality of the mount under which the line dips shows a bad influence.

The length of your head-line is important:

The long line shows that you have a versatile mind. A long line is one that ends beyond the ring finger.

A short line ending under or almost under the long middle finger suggests a one-track mind. This sign has a more emphatic meaning in a long hand than a broad one.

DO YOU HAVE REMARKABLE INSIGHT?
—YOGI SACHIN MAJUMDAR

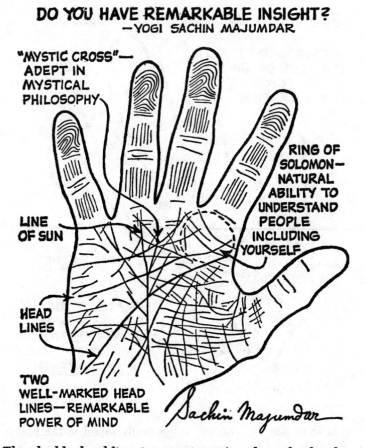

"MYSTIC CROSS"—
ADEPT IN
MYSTICAL
PHILOSOPHY

RING OF
SOLOMON—
NATURAL
ABILITY TO
UNDERSTAND
PEOPLE
INCLUDING
YOURSELF

LINE
OF SUN

HEAD
LINES

TWO
WELL-MARKED HEAD
LINES—REMARKABLE
POWER OF MIND

Sachin Majumdar

The double head-line is sometimes found in the hands of people who are both practical and adept in mystical philosophy. Cheiro had a double head-line.

And here is the interpretation of some unusual head-lines:

Double head-line—the old-fashioned reading of this was "luck in money matters." A later reading points up the qualities of versatility, command of language and the power

ARE YOU AN UNUSUAL PERSON?

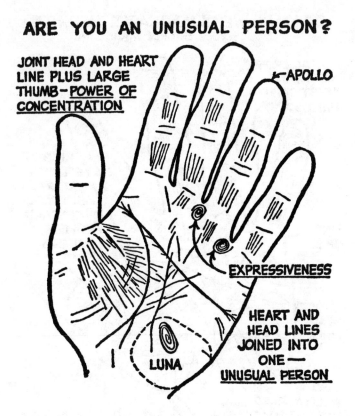

JOINT HEAD AND HEART LINE PLUS LARGE THUMB—POWER OF CONCENTRATION

APOLLO

EXPRESSIVENESS

HEART AND HEAD LINES JOINED INTO ONE — UNUSUAL PERSON

LUNA

to analyze people. This line is generally found in the hands of people who lead two distinctly different lives or follow two fields of activity in which they reveal different sides of their nature or even opposite talents.

Head- and heart-line in one line—always the sign of an unusual person; if you have a large thumb, you have tremendous powers of concentration.

The space between head and heart lines is called the Quadrangle—

If the space between the head-line and the heart-line above it (called the quadrangle) is wide, it indicates broadmindedness; if your quadrangle is narrow, you are strict and set in your ideas. I don't mean that a man with a narrow quadrangle is conventional, but he has his own fixed ideas and sticks to them. I have seen a narrow quadrangle on the hands of an inflexible radical who prided himself on his "tolerant" mind.

CHAPTER XI

THE MAN WITH THE POWER

"Life consists not in holding good cards but in playing those you do hold well."

—Josh Billings.

Below the index finger is the Mount of Jupiter, which is above the Mount of active Mars and divided from it by the life-line. Like all the mounts, this one is named to help you remember it—Jupiter was the ruler of the Roman gods.

This mount and the finger above it show how you wish to deal with other people. Do you want to govern them by running for political office, influence their minds or boss them around? Or maybe you just want to live and let live. Whatever the answer, it will show up on your Mount of Jupiter.

First, let's start with the extremes. A well padded or marked Mount of Jupiter and a long, strong index finger backed up by a large thumb and widely curving life-line are the marks of a born leader. How long is a long, strong index? You have to depend partly on your eye, but the normal length for the index extends to the middle of the tip section of your middle or longest finger (in comparing fingers, it is somewhat more accurate to measure from the back). A very long finger, called the "Forefinger of

Napoleon," will be longer than the ring finger. Fewer than ten persons in a hundred have a finger this long.

A short index with a flat, unmarked Mount of Jupiter shows a desire to take a back seat. Sometimes it indicates a lack of self-respect, especially if the finger is very short —for example, if it reaches the beginning of the tip section of the middle finger.

Either a long, strong, out-leaning finger or a high or much lined mount under it shows a desire to lead in some way. Usually these signs are accompanied by a normal thumb. If the thumb is small, you know immediately that the person has a problem: he desires to lead without the strength of purpose to carry through his plans. The general markings on your hand will show whether or not the problem is serious.

If you hold your hand tensely and your lines look tortured, it is indeed disturbing.

This combination of a long index and short thumb appeared in the beautifully marked hands of a teacher who intended to become a nun. She felt that what she had to offer could only be developed once she had the spiritual support of a group as well as her personal religion.

This brings us to another quality that goes with a well developed Mount of Jupiter—a strong feeling for religion, a sense that power should be spiritual as well as worldly. This is emphasized in hands with conic or pointed fingers.

If your Mount of Jupiter under your index finger is roundly padded or has several rising lines, a well marked star or a trident on it, you possess the creative power of leadership and a desire to influence other people.

A developed mount and a short index finger are sometimes found in a hand with a long ring finger, suggesting that this person wants to assert himself through self-expression rather than through any sort of ordinary leadership.

An undeveloped mount with a long, strong finger is the sign of an ambitious person who is extremely active but not inclined to originate any new ways of doing things. As a committee chairman, he would preside effectively but not make many suggestions.

Left from the link of palmistry with astrology is the description of the "Jupiterian Hand." The Mount of Jupiter may actually be found developed in many shapes of hands, but, as you will see, the hand shape called "Jupiterian"

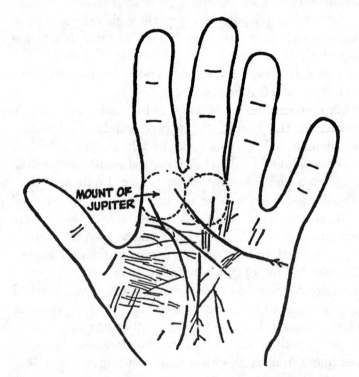

MOUNT OF JUPITER →

When Jupiter is set high on the hand, it emphasizes ambition.

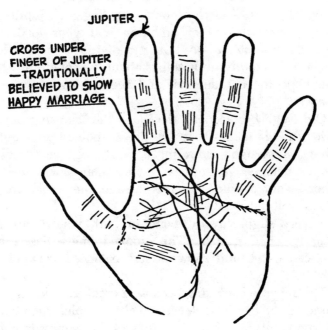

JUPITER

CROSS UNDER
FINGER OF JUPITER
—TRADITIONALLY
BELIEVED TO SHOW
HAPPY MARRIAGE

would be especially likely to belong to a quick-thinking, practical and ambitious man—the kind who might become a recognized leader.

The "Jupiterian Hand" is thick and massive with fairly long but thick, smooth, square-tipped fingers. The index finger alone is conic-tipped. The thumb ranges from normal to large with a large tip section. Both Mounts of Mars are fairly large, giving the palm a somewhat circular shape. The palm is pale red. Of course, it goes without saying that the mount and finger of Jupiter are large. An intellectual variation of the "Jupiterian Hand" might be paler with lower Mounts of Mars.

Because of its massiveness and thick fingers, this hand indicates a love of comfort and plenty, usually associated with a highly developed Mount of Jupiter.

While the size of the mount and finger of Jupiter indicates your degree of ambition and your leadership potential, the shape, position and divisions of your forefinger tell us more subtle things about the sphere in which you hope to be influential and the quality of your influence.

Old English books call the index the "showing finger." A long index means that you like to point things out to others. A straight index means that you see things in proper perspective and can point them out clearly to others. Your attitude toward life and the world around you is well balanced.

A very slight inward bend in both your index and little finger is normal. The crooked finger has a pronounced curve and shows a less balanced view of the world.

This may be confusing because a crooked index is often found on the hands of clever and able people. One reading interprets this bent finger as a sign of shrewdness in realizing ambitions. It is often the finger of the expert who has been defined as "a man far from home who knows more and more about less and less." The expert doesn't always have a well-rounded view of the world, because he may be so busy studying his own field that he may neglect to study anything else. He may still be an extremely useful and clever person. He is very shrewd in his own field.

In a clumsy hand with scrambled lines, the crooked index shows a decidedly unbalanced view of the world and hence misguided ambition. A man with such an index may find that his "success" consists of having almost enough money to pay the bills he wouldn't have if he weren't so "successful."

If the tip section of your index finger is the longest of the three inside sections, you want to be a leader in some abstract and idealistic way. You want to influence the ethics or ideals of those around you rather than influence their actions directly. This might be the hand of the religious reformer or the abstract intellectual.

If the middle section of your finger is the longest, you want to influence other men's actions directly. Your ambitions might be political.

If your palm section is by far the longest (it is often slightly longer than the other two), your ambitions are very down-to-earth. You want personal power and the symbol of it—money. You want to be boss. If the sections are balanced, the balance is reflected in your thinking.

SOLOMON'S RING

The Ring of Solomon, the line associated with the Mount of Jupiter, also shows that you have the power to understand and influence other people. This power seems to be both intuitive and intellectual and the line usually accompanies a high intelligence (lack of the "ring" certainly doesn't suggest a low intelligence).

In its strongest form, the "ring" goes all the way around the index finger and is marked on the back of the hand as well as the front. Sometimes it is a double or triple ring.

According to the old reading of this line, the subject had a talent for occult studies. It was also called a sign of divination.

The name "Ring of Solomon" is a reminder of the ancient days when hand-reading was related to magic. In the mythology of magic, Solomon was regarded as probably the greatest magician of all time, and he was said to have been the first to collect many of the spells and charms listed in the *grimoires* or grammars of magical procedure.

Stories say he had a ring of brass and iron joined together, engraved with a magical seal and set with the jewels of the angels of the four elements. By means of

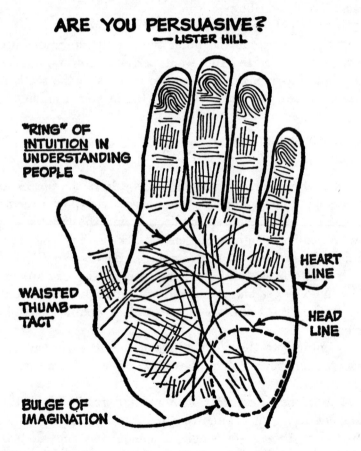

ARE YOU PERSUASIVE?
—LISTER HILL

"RING" OF INTUITION IN UNDERSTANDING PEOPLE

WAISTED THUMB— TACT

BULGE OF IMAGINATION

HEART LINE

HEAD LINE

When these signs combine with the Ring of Solomon, as in Sen. Lister Hill's hand, persuasiveness is suggested.

this ring, he subdued spirits and made them do his bidding. It also gave him the power to understand the speech of birds and animals.

If you have the Ring of Solomon on your hand, you won't be able to understand the songs of the birds, but through intelligence and intuition you'll understand not only what people say, but much of what they leave unsaid.

CHAPTER XII

YOUR FATE AND WEIGHT

"As knowledge increases, wonder deepens."
—Charles Morgan.

Next to the Mount of Jupiter and under the long middle finger is the Mount of Saturn. Medium high or marked with one or two well formed lines and combined with a large middle finger (or a middle finger that draws the other fingers toward it), this mount shows a studious or philosophic turn of mind and a love for the solitude of nature. The Saturnian is also inclined to be a cautious person, and he is often a skeptic.

If this mount is high or covered with a number of disorderly lines, or if the finger above it is large and massive—out of all proportion to the other fingers—it indicates fits of depression. It also suggests someone who may be so preoccupied with bookish interests that he doesn't take the time to be orderly.

It must have been a Saturnian who said, "He who spends his time reading books has a disorderly attic." Abraham Lincoln, who has been called Saturnian, used to leave his law office in Illinois so messy that seeds sprouted in the dust.

You will often see that the mounts of Saturn and Jupiter are high, padded and linked together. Add a large thumb, and you have all the signs of the active philosopher, the man who wants to convince others of his philosophy or get ahead in the world through serious studies. If you find this combination of Saturn and Jupiter with a small or bent-in thumb, it is a likely sign of morbid pride.

If your middle finger is extremely short and pointed, you may be irresponsible. A normal finger is about half a tip section taller than the ring and index fingers. A slightly shorter finger may suggest someone who depends more on intuition than intellect. The short middle finger serves as a religious symbol, and is supposed to be one of the marks on the hands of Buddha.

Few of us ordinary mortals have such infallible intuition that we can do without a somewhat developed intellect to steer us. So with ordinary mortals, a short middle finger (almost the same length as the index and ring) suggests a possible lack of balance.

A developed Mount of Saturn, high or marked with lines, is (as you might imagine) emphasized in a long, rectangular and bony hand that often has knotty fingers underlining an inward trend of mind and a philosophic streak.

This "Saturnian hand" is usually found on people who love science and such earthy, basically lonely pursuits as farming or mining. Intellectuals with this type of hand love to study philosophy or psychology and prefer classical music or progressive jazz to more popular music.

The funniest humor has a core of serious truth. When we find life bleak and depressing, we need to keep joking to bear life at all. Therefore, it's not surprising that many humorists are Saturnians.

Saturn may be found in a broad hand, especially in

combination with the Mount of Jupiter or the Mount of Mars.

The middle finger shows how studious or down-to-earth qualities are used: if the tip section is the longest, an

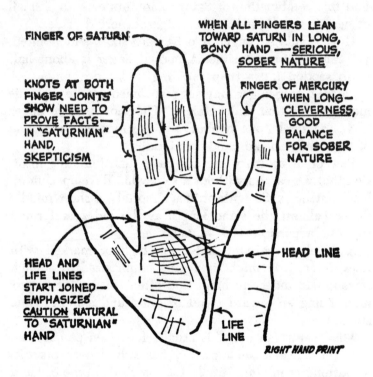

FINGER OF SATURN

WHEN ALL FINGERS LEAN TOWARD SATURN IN LONG, BONY HAND — SERIOUS, SOBER NATURE

KNOTS AT BOTH FINGER JOINTS SHOW NEED TO PROVE FACTS — IN "SATURNIAN" HAND, SKEPTICISM

FINGER OF MERCURY WHEN LONG — CLEVERNESS, GOOD BALANCE FOR SOBER NATURE

HEAD LINE

HEAD AND LIFE LINES START JOINED — EMPHASIZES CAUTION NATURAL TO "SATURNIAN" HAND

LIFE LINE

RIGHT HAND PRINT

interest in philosophy is evident; if the middle section, we note an interest in such useful studies as science or agriculture. When the palm section is the longest of the three, it's a sign of concentration and staying power—and sometimes avarice.

THE LINE OF SATURN (FATE-LINE)

Under the serious finger of Saturn is the most controversial line in hand-reading. Everyone believes it means something very important, but *what* does it mean?

Desbarrolles called this line, in its lengthy, well-marked form, a sign of good fortune. The born ruler was said to have it—straight as an arrow from his wrist to the center

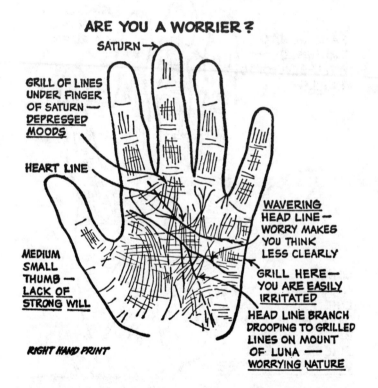

ARE YOU A WORRIER?

SATURN →

GRILL OF LINES
UNDER FINGER
OF SATURN —
DEPRESSED
MOODS

HEART LINE

MEDIUM
SMALL
THUMB —
LACK OF
STRONG WILL

RIGHT HAND PRINT

WAVERING
HEAD LINE —
WORRY MAKES
YOU THINK
LESS CLEARLY

GRILL HERE —
YOU ARE EASILY
IRRITATED

HEAD LINE BRANCH
DROOPING TO GRILLED
LINES ON MOUNT
OF LUNA —
WORRYING NATURE

Tangle of disorderly lines under Saturn shows discouraged moods. Other signs of a tendency to worry are often found in the same hand.

of his Mount of Saturn. Cheiro said much the same thing, but he admitted that he once found such a line in the hands of a tramp. Both writers computed time on the fate-line, beginning with childhood near the wrist and ending with old age near the fingers.

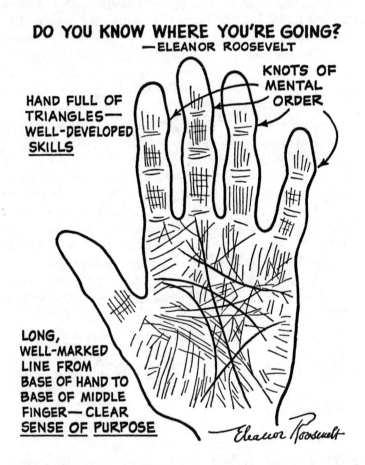

DO YOU KNOW WHERE YOU'RE GOING?
—ELEANOR ROOSEVELT

KNOTS OF MENTAL ORDER

HAND FULL OF TRIANGLES— WELL-DEVELOPED SKILLS

LONG, WELL-MARKED LINE FROM BASE OF HAND TO BASE OF MIDDLE FINGER— CLEAR SENSE OF PURPOSE

Eleanor Roosevelt

Well-marked fate-line from wrist to middle finger is usually seen with other signs of self-assurance.

Other writers have thought that the fate-line represents inherited outer circumstances or social adaptability, or that it showed the naturally productive moments in a man's life.

In my experience, a well-marked fate-line shows a clear sense of purpose. It is almost always more clearly marked on a conic, philosophic or psychic hand than on an elementary or square hand. Yet the square-hander is often successful because he is practical, hard-working and inclined to aim for the goals that are accepted as normal and proper by the people around him. This would be a problem only if he grew up among people with a warped sense of direction.

Since a clear, well-marked fate-line shows a strong sense of purpose, you see it on the hands of many people who are successful, both in material ways and as human beings. A refugee I know has been driven from her home twice, but has come through the experience alive and a fine person. She has a long, well-marked fate-line.

Whatever the explanation, the traditional meanings for the fate-line seem to work very well. Here they are:

No fate-line—you can only achieve success through hard work.

A badly marked line—you suffer many ups and downs.

WHERE YOUR FATE-LINE BEGINS

The starting place of your fate-line is also important:

Starts inside the life-line—you succeed with the help of relatives. The person with this line often feels he has received too much help and hasn't been allowed freedom to develop during his youth.

*Starts from the center of the palm near the wrist—*you'll succeed through personal effort.

*Starts from the Mount of Moon—*you'll succeed through the help of those outside the family or you depend on the whim of the public. When your fate-line starts here, it emphasizes the imaginative area of your hand. Thus you often see it on the hands of writers, actors and others who depend for their success on the help of those who are less temperamental than they.

*The line begins well above the wrist—*on a long hand, this indicates no definite purpose until later in life, perhaps

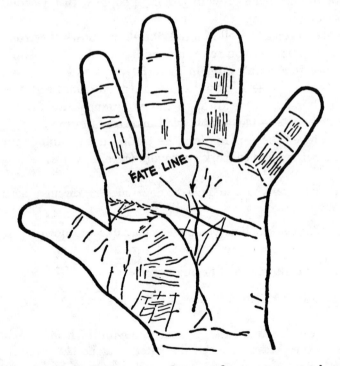

Wavy fate-line shows many changes due to its owner's uncertain sense of direction.

during your middle years. On a broad hand it has less meaning.

THE END OF YOUR FATE-LINE

The place where your fate-line ends is very significant:

If it ends low in your hand, below your head-line, with no new fate-line or "sun-line" under your ring finger beginning

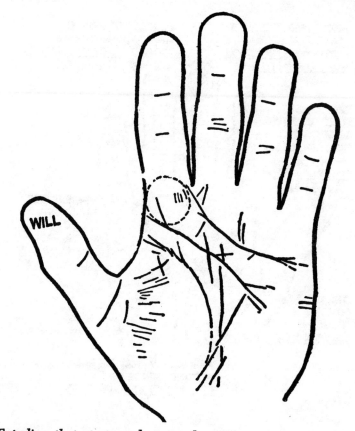

Fate-line that starts and stops, then starts again in another place means (by tradition) a change.

above it: traditional reading—the end of smooth sailing because of mental blundering; latest reading—if your hand is long, you may have bumpy going because you have no purpose or plan; if it's broad, you will work out your own fate.

If your fate-line ends and a new line begins—this indicates

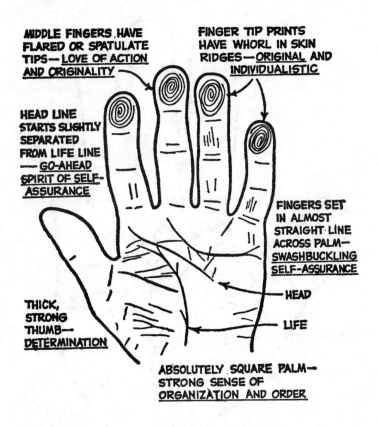

The hand with virtually no fate-line may show other qualities that lead to success.

a change; if it ends high on a mount (traditional meaning), you will enjoy smooth sailing right through old age.

Ends on the Mount of Jupiter—your life is ruled by ambition; you will probably succeed.

OTHER DISTINCTIVE MARKS

A fate-line cut by many horizontal lines from the Mount of Venus—you'll have a bumpy ride through life because you are inclined to worry about this and that.

A wavy fate-line—your life will undergo constant changes; many small lines rising from your fate-line—you are hopeful and ambitious.

Many small downward lines—you are easily discouraged; when branches from your fate-line extend to a mount or the line rises high in your hand and then curves toward the mount—you will use your abilities as indicated by the mount, for example:

  Jupiter, ambition;
  Saturn, serious studies;
  Apollo (under your ring finger),
        self-expression;
  Mercury (under your little fin-
        ger), practical clever-
        ness.

CHAPTER XIII

STYLE AND PERSONALITY

"To the question 'what is art?' we answer: 'That whereby forms are transmuted into style.'"
—André Malraux.

When the Mount of Apollo (under the ring finger) is high, crowned with a star or marked with one or two straight clear lines, it promises a sense of style.

If you have a developed Mount of Apollo, then whatever you do—whether you sell cheese, recite Shakespeare, paint pictures or rob banks—you act in a stylish, dashing way. You are a spontaneous person. If you are smart, people describe you as brilliant. A not-so-smart person with this mount may be dashing or, at the very least (and worst), flashy.

The high Mount of Apollo signifies a great love of the beautiful and colorful, the ability to enjoy life and to convey that joy to others.

If your ring finger or finger of Apollo is longer than your index finger, you may be more interested in enjoying and sometimes creating the beauty around you than in dominating other people. When combined with a short thumb, the long ring finger indicates someone who finds

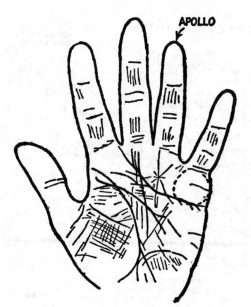

Star under the ring finger goes with a sense of style.

harmonious and beautiful surroundings as necessary as food and drink.

If you have a long ring finger (especially one with a high or starred Mount of Apollo beneath it) combined with a long thumb, you like to use your brilliance creatively—act, paint, write or do any job where success depends on dazzling the people with whom you deal.

A long ring finger, almost as long as the middle finger and considerably longer than the index, usually goes with artistic "temperament." Maria Callas has a long ring finger like this.

Especially when it is joined with a short thumb, the long ring finger hints at a tendency toward gambling—a double-or-nothing turn of mind. With a long thumb, the gambler has a better chance to win.

DO YOU HAVE HIDDEN TALENT?

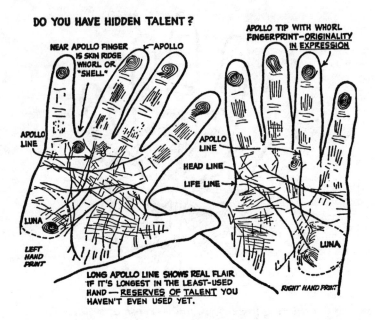

Producer-playwright George Abbott has creative talent marked in his hands by Apollo lines from the Mount of Luna and by "shell" markings on the Apollo mounts.

The importance of the mount and finger is emphasized in a hand whose whole form shows spontaneity and love of beauty and receptivity.

The hand is usually almost conic, but sometimes the fingertips are square. The Mount of Venus is inclined to be large, giving an oval shape to the palm. The fingers may have the knots of order nearest the palm but, beyond these, they are smooth. The thumb is usually turned out at the tip because most stylish, dashing people are adaptable and at least a little bit extravagant.

If the tip section of your ring finger is much longer than the other two sections, you love ideal beauty.

When your middle section is the longest, you have the ability to use your sense of style practically.

If your palm section is long and fleshy, you probably love luxury.

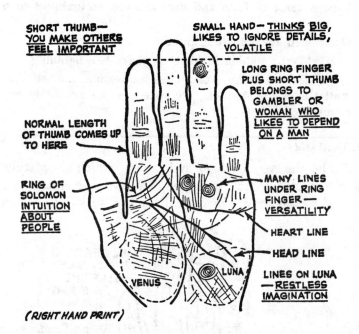

SHORT THUMB—
YOU MAKE OTHERS
FEEL IMPORTANT

SMALL HAND—THINKS BIG,
LIKES TO IGNORE DETAILS,
VOLATILE

LONG RING FINGER
PLUS SHORT THUMB
BELONGS TO
GAMBLER OR
WOMAN WHO
LIKES TO DEPEND
ON A MAN

NORMAL LENGTH
OF THUMB COMES UP
TO HERE

RING OF
SOLOMON
INTUITION
ABOUT
PEOPLE

MANY LINES
UNDER RING
FINGER—
VERSATILITY

HEART LINE

HEAD LINE

LINES ON LUNA
—RESTLESS
IMAGINATION

VENUS   LUNA

(RIGHT HAND PRINT)

Short thumb plus long ring-finger usually belongs to a gambler. In a feminine hand, this combination leads to the woman who likes to lean on a man.

The crooked ring finger suggests a kink in your ability to enjoy life. Sometimes it belongs to a person who gives up his own personal enjoyment for others.

When your ring and middle finger lean toward each other, it suggests a conflict between your sense of serious responsibility and desire for self-expression and the spontaneous enjoyment of life.

POSSIBLE TIPS ON THE RING FINGER

What kind of tip do you have on your ring finger?

Square—sense of form and line; are you an architect or a builder?

Conic—you are quickly inspired.

Pointed—your sudden inspirations strike like lightning.

Spatulate—you have a talent for expressing yourself dramatically, in pantomime, etc. Are you an actor, by any chance?

THE APOLLO OR SUN-LINE

Under the Apollo finger and mount, which show style, is one of the happiest lines you can have—the Apollo line or, as it was traditionally called, the luck-line. When

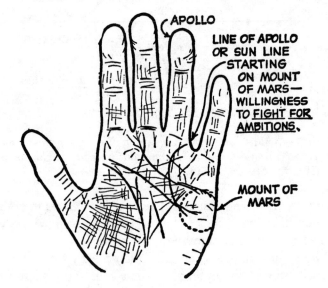

APOLLO

LINE OF APOLLO
OR SUN LINE
STARTING
ON MOUNT
OF MARS—
WILLINGNESS
TO FIGHT FOR
AMBITIONS.

MOUNT OF
MARS

clearly marked, this line is a symbol of self-realization. It seems to go with the mind's intuitive and creative power.

You find the Apollo line on the hands of writers who can always express exactly what they mean or business-men who always seize the right opportunity with such seeming ease that it looks like luck.

A long, well-marked Apollo line doesn't necessarily belong to someone rich or famous, but if his hand is well-balanced he has the intuitive power to achieve his deepest

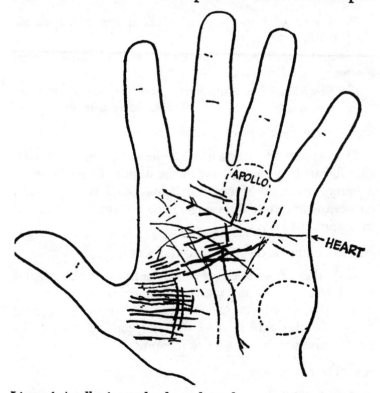

Line of Apollo from the heart-line shows creative power if combined with a well-marked fate-line lower in the hand.

personal desires. In a distorted hand, it merely signifies a desire to show off.

The Apollo line is frequently unmarked on a broad hand. This person succeeds through steady, hard work rather than brilliant flashes of inspirations.

STARTING PLACES FOR THE APOLLO LINE

The wrist—some form of artistic talent.

The Mount of Moon—you show you are blessed with a creative imagination; actors who can "create" a part often have this line.

The Mount of Mars—you show a willingness to struggle for self-fulfillment.

The center of the hand—(traditional reading) you'll succeed after some tribulation.

The heart-line—this is the usual place for the line to start, and it means that you'll enjoy success after hard work.

ENDING OF THE APOLLO LINE

The Apollo line always ends near the base of your ring finger. If it curves toward the middle finger or sends a branch there, it shows the influence of wisdom. If it curves toward your little finger, you will use your talents in a practical way.

OTHER ASPECTS OF THE APOLLO LINE

More than three lines on your Mount of Apollo suggest a Jack-of-all-trades and master of none.

A well-marked star at the end of the line suggests creative ability and style—a winning combination. A trident at the end has the same meaning.

AN OLD TRADITION

If you have three lines on the mount, you will never lack money.

CHAPTER XIV

THAT EXTRA SOMETHING

*"Take him up on top of the mountain, tie him to a tree,
and he'll come back with ten dollars."*
—North Carolina mountain saying.

The Mount of Mercury under the little finger endows a
man with that "extra something"—the sure insight of the
investor who beats the market; the flash of understanding
that gives the scientist a new answer before he even
realizes how he discovered it; the quick wit of the debater.

Like the Mount of Apollo, the Mount of Mercury signifies intuitive abilities; but they differ in the way you use
them. The large or well-marked Mount of Mercury belongs to the man of the world. He is shrewd, and unless he
has the Mount of Apollo too (a common combination), he
would rather use his eloquence to win legal cases or an
election than write poetry. Science appeals to him as a
practical way in which to use his intuitive gifts. He can
be a very successful businessman.

If you wanted one word for the Mount of Mercury, it
would be "clever." If the mount juts out at the side of the
hand, the owner of a sensitive hand would have the sort
of quicksilver mind that would make him not only clever

but unpredictable. This jutting-out in a practical hand underlines intuitive business sense.

As you might expect, the Mount of Mercury plays an important role in hands with fairly short, often smooth

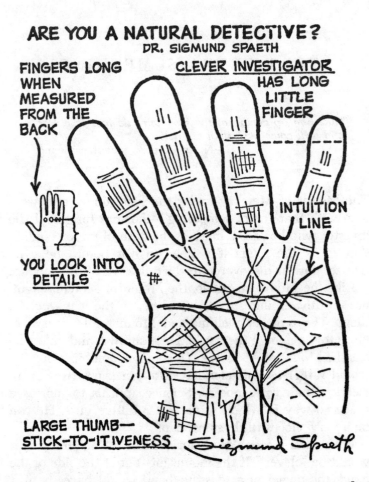

ARE YOU A NATURAL DETECTIVE?
DR. SIGMUND SPAETH

FINGERS LONG WHEN MEASURED FROM THE BACK

YOU LOOK INTO DETAILS

CLEVER INVESTIGATOR HAS LONG LITTLE FINGER

INTUITION LINE

LARGE THUMB— STICK-TO-ITIVENESS

Sigmund Spaeth

Long little finger lends the support of cleverness to any other qualities shown in the hand.

fingers that emphasize quick thinking. The palm is often long and shaped like a top-heavy trapezoid.

It is the long little finger that makes the Mount of Mercury important, even when it is flat. The finger also tells us how you exercise your cleverness. The long little finger, even with a low or flat mount, belongs to an expressive person. He can find the right word or, more

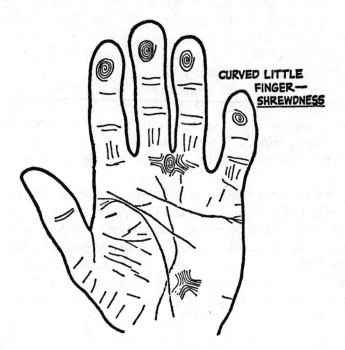

CURVED LITTLE
FINGER—
SHREWDNESS

correctly, the right hundred words to express himself. If he is an actor, he can, as the expression goes, "act with his back."

The long little finger with a high mount indicates shrewdness, exceptional wit and tact. If the little finger is very long (if it extends as far as the nail of the ring finger) you should be on the alert—this person can deceive you.

Unless it is set very low on the hand, a long little finger is one that reaches the fingernail on the ring finger. Normally, your "Mercury" finger reaches the beginning line of the tip section of your ring finger. A short little finger would not extend that far.

A crooked finger with a high mount belongs to a person who can easily fool the people around him. Such a person may be a detective or intelligence agent or a crook. A slightly crooked finger emphasizes shrewdness without hinting at underhand practices.

A short finger with a high mount is in the hand of an impetuous and usually cheerful person. Together with a small, narrow Mount of Venus, it suggests someone who would be perfectly happy unmarried.

The low-set little finger is a sign of diffidence and shyness.

In a woman's hands you will often see a normal or even long little finger with a mount that juts out at the side of her hand. When she joins her fingers, her little finger and its mount are set so low that the finger *looks* short. The woman with such a little finger is both clever and shy. She's the sort who persuades her husband to see the mayor about a new public playground because she's shy about visiting him herself.

THE SECTIONS OF THE LITTLE FINGER

When your tip section is the longest, it means that you are eloquent or at least you love to talk.

When your middle section is the longest, you make practical use of your intuition and cleverness (are you a scientist?).

When your palm section is the longest, you are a shrewd customer and bear watching!

How is the tip of your little finger shaped?

If it's square, you love form.

If it's conic, you may be musical.

If it's pointed, you have a lightning wit.

If it's spatulate, you are probably inventive (are you a mechanic?).

AN OLD TRADITION

The horizontal lines on the side of the hand between the little finger and the heart-line below it indicate the number of times you will marry. If tiny vertical lines touch these horizontal lines, each means a child. The French call all the horizontal lines the "lines of sex appeal."

ANOTHER KIND OF LOVE

The heart-line begins at the outer edge of the hand below the Mount of Mercury. This line shows the ability to love, though not through an overflow of physical warmth, vitality and high spirits. That aspect of love is revealed on the Mount of Venus. Running, as the heart-line does, largely in the intuitive side of the hand, the heart-line shows the qualities of intuitive rapport and sympathy—the qualities of our emotions rather than the depth of our passions.

Normally the heart-line runs nearly as far below the ring finger as the length of the tip section of that finger. If it is much higher in the hand, it indicates that you lack subtlety and depth in your feelings. In other words, you are the sort of person who might sing, "I told you I loved you—now get out!"

If the heart-line is more or less straight, it suggests a more idealistic and mental type of love, like the couple who "looked adoringly at each other more than they kissed." If the heart-line has a definite curve, it suggests the opposite. These people need to express their love as concretely as possible.

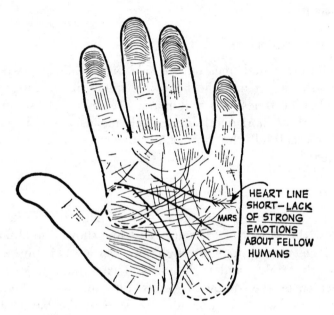

HEART LINE
SHORT—LACK
OF STRONG
EMOTIONS
ABOUT FELLOW
HUMANS

MARS

If this line is short, not running beyond the middle of the long middle finger, it suggests that love, for you, is not a matter of rapport and insight but either an over-flowing of physical warmth, if the Mount of Venus is high, or a result purely of intellectual respect, if the head-line is long and well-marked.

At the other extreme, if your heart-line reaches all the way across your hand to the far side of the Mount of

Jupiter, you will feel the joys of great love but will also be at the mercy of your emotions.

If your heart-line ends under the center of your index finger, you are inclined to expect so much of the people

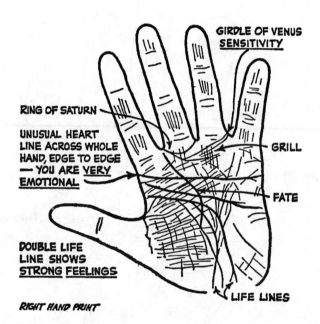

Other markings may emphasize the super-emotional nature of the person with a heart-line that embraces the whole hand. In a narrow hand, this suggests jealousy.

you love that you are frequently disappointed. When your friends fall off their pedestals, *you* are the one who gets hurt.

A heart-line that curves up between the index and middle fingers suggests a person who is realistic in his

affection for other people and therefore usually happy
in love.

When your heart-line ends in a number of forks, you
are a warm-hearted and emotional person.

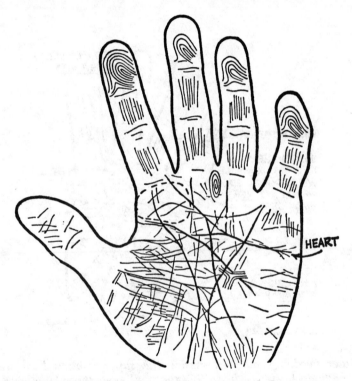

*Heart-line that ends under the index finger belongs to a man
who wants to idealize the people he loves.*

When your heart-line joins the head- and life-lines, you
are completely oblivious to danger. Desbarrolles describes people of your sort as the kind who walk along the
edge of cliffs blindfolded. You incline toward extremes of
intelligence—brilliance or feeble-mindedness.

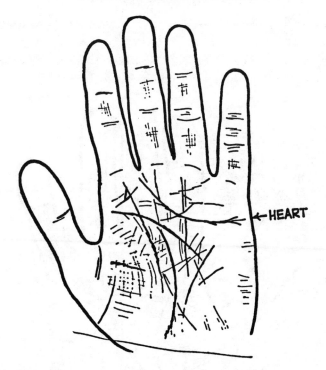

Heart-line curving up between index and middle finger shows practical, realistic affections.

THE GIRDLE OF VENUS

Above the heart-line and more or less parallel to it is a line nearer the base of the fingers that sometimes circles the middle and ring fingers. This is the Girdle of Venus.

If you have this line, you are high-strung and emotionally responsive—qualities that can be good or bad, depending on how they are used. When this line is triple or quadruple, it means you have trouble controlling your emotions. Sometimes it indicates hysteria.

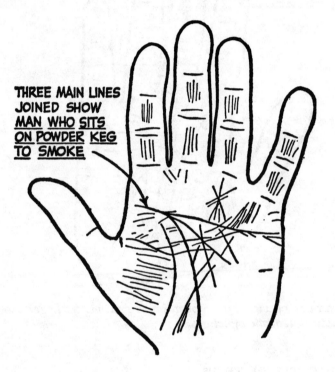

THREE MAIN LINES
JOINED SHOW
MAN WHO SITS
ON POWDER KEG
TO SMOKE

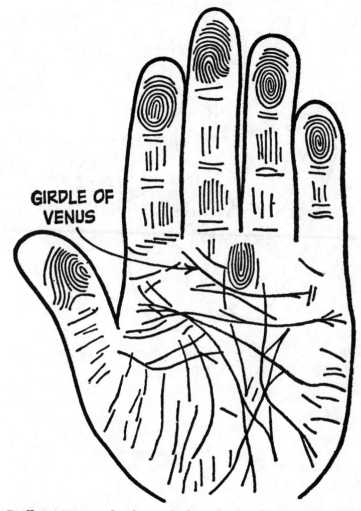

GIRDLE OF VENUS

Girdle of Venus, clearly marked in the hand of author Henry Miller, is often found in the hands of writers and artists who must feel things deeply in order to express them movingly.

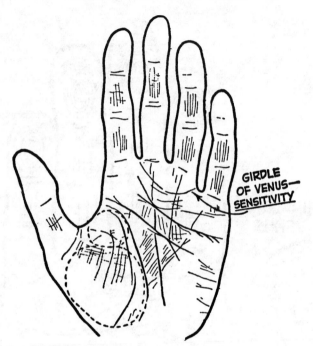

GIRDLE
OF VENUS—
SENSITIVITY

*Double or triple Girdle of Venus belongs to a person who is
too sensitive for his own comfort.*

CHAPTER XV

STAYING POWER

*"The art of living is more like that of wrestling than of
dancing; the main thing is to stand firm and be ready for
an unforeseen attack."*

—Marcus Aurelius.

If your Mount of Mars, which is under the Mount of
Mercury, is well padded in proportion to the rest of your
hand, you have the power to bear up under difficulties,
no matter how trying.

The quality of this mount is best illustrated by the
ancient story of the poor couple who had such a beautiful
and promising baby that they scraped together their
pennies and went off to the soothsayer to find out what
wonderful future lay in store for the child.

"When he's two," the soothsayer said, "he'll have
measles; when he's eight, he'll have smallpox and lose his
complexion; when he's fourteen, he'll scald himself and
lose all his hair; and when he's eighteen, he'll marry the
ugliest and poorest girl in the village."

"Won't anything wonderful happen to him?" the parents
asked.

"Yes," said the soothsayer, "when he's twenty something
very wonderful will happen. He'll get used to it."

When you can take your troubles calmly and bravely, you are a lucky person indeed.

If your Mount of passive Mars under Mercury is highly padded and the Mount of active Mars under Jupiter is also high, you are a person of action who gets what he wants by sheer energy, persistence and determination. You are a fighter.

If your hand brings out all the strongest qualities of the two Mounts of Mars, both passive and active, and suggests the indomitable fighter, it is firm and square-palmed with square-shaped fingers. The outside edge of your hand is

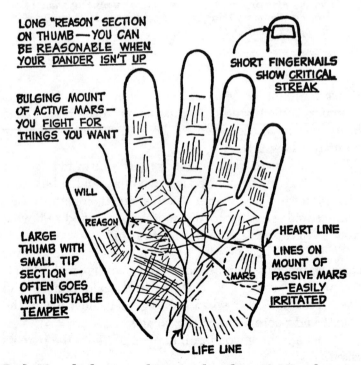

LONG "REASON" SECTION ON THUMB—YOU CAN BE REASONABLE WHEN YOUR DANDER ISN'T UP

SHORT FINGERNAILS SHOW CRITICAL STREAK

BULGING MOUNT OF ACTIVE MARS—YOU FIGHT FOR THINGS YOU WANT

WILL

REASON

LARGE THUMB WITH SMALL TIP SECTION—OFTEN GOES WITH UNSTABLE TEMPER

HEART LINE

LINES ON MOUNT OF PASSIVE MARS—EASILY IRRITATED

MARS

LIFE LINE

Both Mars high, many lines in the plain of Mars between them, plus other signs, add up to a violent temper.

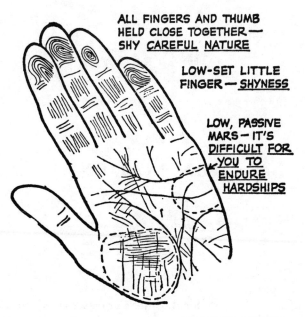

ALL FINGERS AND THUMB
HELD CLOSE TOGETHER—
SHY CAREFUL NATURE

LOW-SET LITTLE
FINGER — SHYNESS

LOW, PASSIVE
MARS — IT'S
DIFFICULT FOR
YOU TO
ENDURE
HARDSHIPS

RIGHT HAND PRINT

Low mount of passive Mars is emphasized by other signs.

highly padded and forms a right angle at the base of the hand. Your fingers are big and probably stiff and straight. The Mounts of Mars and Venus are large. The lines in your hand are broad and red, and your palm is probably red. The Martian fighter is not always a boxer or soldier; he may be a crusading newspaperman.

The space between the two Mounts of Mars is called the Plain of Mars. If both mounts are high, the plain is full of disorderly lines and a number of lines are found on the passive mount, you'd better watch that temper of yours!

On the other hand, if your passive mount is high, firm and unlined, you are able to control your temper. And you can control it if you have a well-shaped thumb, preferably one that is slightly long.

CHAPTER XVI

IMAGINATION

"Exaltation is the going
Of an inland soul to sea."
—Emily Dickinson.

The Mount of Luna, located near your wrist on the side of your hand below the little finger, shows how imaginative you are and (to a certain extent) how you use your imagination.

Hand-readers list many qualities revealed by Luna, including daydreams, a love of the sea, a love of mystery, exaltation, a large vocabulary, contemplation, the creative spark of genius, lying, coldness and selfishness.

The imaginative person can create images and symbols within his own mind that seem almost as real as the objects he can touch and smell and taste and see. If he passes that "almost" point and his inner world becomes more real than the world around him, his imagination can make him cold and selfish. He may retreat into his own world of fancy and ignore other people. On the other hand, he may become so unable to see truth that he tells lies without even realizing it. Young children who are very imaginative often do this and are furious and hurt that their parents won't believe there really is a dragon waiting at the front door.

Fortunately, as we grow older, most of us can use our imaginations in a constructive way. Words are symbols for

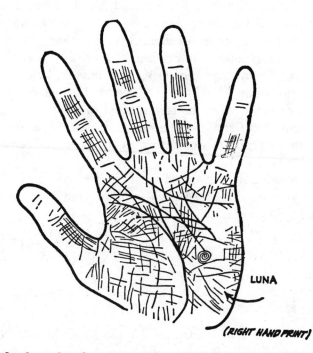

LUNA

(RIGHT HAND PRINT)

In the long hand, imagination is usually shown by a long, kidney-shaped Mount of Luna marked by lines. By tradition, vertical lines show sea voyages.

things, and a large vocabulary depends on imagination, though not every imaginative person has a good vocabulary.

The day dreamer may dream about strawberry short-cake or the beautiful blonde who lives down the street, or he may compose novels or operas or paint pictures. A man who played the stock market had one of the largest Mounts of Luna I ever saw.

If your hand bulges noticeably in the Luna area or the mount is clearly marked by lines, you have a strong imagination. This is also true if the mount is red or one of the major lines of the hand crosses it. A skin whorl on the mount is the sign of an exuberant imagination.

If your Luna mount bulges near the wrist or most of its marks are down near the wrist, you have a kinesthetic imagination, one in which the images formed by your mind are likely to be in terms of physical feeling and movement. Very sensuous people and those who are attuned to such rhythms of nature as the tides and seasons have this kind of Luna.

If your Mount of Luna is most marked on the higher part of your hand that is nearer to Mars, your imagination is more sublimated.

The way you use your imagination is also shown by your other developed mounts and the general shape of your hand.

LONG, FLEXIBLE HAND

If you have a long, slender, supple hand, your receptive imagination is a great source of enjoyment. But for real fulfillment, you must constantly experience beauty in nature or art.

If your Luna is well-marked but does not bulge with high padding, you are probably an interpretive artist rather than a creator of new thought. You might be a fashion designer or a water-colorist. You probably have a knack for arranging flowers. In a hand such as yours, Luna is long and kidney-shaped and marked by lines.

If the mount is covered with a tangle of lines, the person with a receptive imagination finds it hard not to go over and over his worries in his mind's eye, as a squirrel goes around and around in a wheel. The mount marked by a few clear lines shows a happy use of the imagination.

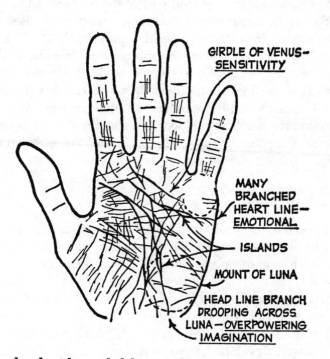

GIRDLE OF VENUS—
SENSITIVITY

MANY
BRANCHED
HEART LINE—
EMOTIONAL

ISLANDS

MOUNT OF LUNA

HEAD LINE BRANCH
DROOPING ACROSS
LUNA—OVERPOWERING
IMAGINATION

In a hand with tangled lines, a branch of the head-line to Luna or strong markings on Luna show an overpowering imagination.

If Luna bulges noticeably, it is a sign of creative push. Many actors, for example, have long, slender hands with Luna and Venus bulging.

LONG, BONY HAND

If you have a long, bony hand with Luna highly developed, your strong imagination is still a source of escape and personal enjoyment. But a large thumb generally rides herd over it. Dreams and imaginings tend to be used as raw material for rationally decided projects. If the fingers have knots at both joints, the imagination finds its outlet in philosophy or science or some other field where system and order are more important than spontaneous inspiration. If Luna is flat but emphasized by lines, the owner of these knotty hands should avoid the inclination to express himself in a pedantic way, using long words even when it's clearer to use short words.

BROAD HAND

If you have a broad, firm, clearly marked hand, you are sure to put your imagination to practical use, especially if you have square fingers. You can cook imaginative and probably spicy dishes, paint pictures that sell or write clearly organized books. If you are in politics, you're working on new and better legislation.

If you have hands that are broad, fleshy and very soft with a well developed Luna, you are a daydreamer. But a large thumb indicates that you have the ability to turn dreams to practical use. Let's suppose that you have spatulate fingertips. This means that you are mentally active, though physically lazy.

If you have very small hands with a developed Luna, your imagination is strong, vivid, impulsive and usually original.

UNDERDEVELOPED LUNA

If your Luna is not curved out at the side of your hand or padded but is bony and flat, you may have so little imagination that it is hard for you to see the other fellow's point of view. Then you must guard against hurting others unintentionally through lack of insight.

However, you may be happier than the imaginative person because you will not feel that you are missing something out of life, and so you will have little desire for the unattainable.

If the Mount of Luna in the hand you use most has a lot of marks but the main lines are more clearly marked and the mount in your other hand is higher, you have had such painful experiences that you have retreated into the world of your imagination and neglected to develop your more active talents. If you take up some craft or art form as a hobby, you will begin to harmonize your activity and imagination.

LUNA INTENSIFIED

If you have short and smooth conic or pointed fingers, the Mount of Luna has much influence over your personality, as you might expect.

With a hand of this sort that is also soft, white and fleshy with a short thumb and fingertips so close as to overlap each other, the imagination is so strong as to be overwhelming. If you have a hand like this, you are a creature of whim and caprice. You must beware of becoming the victim of an overactive imagination.

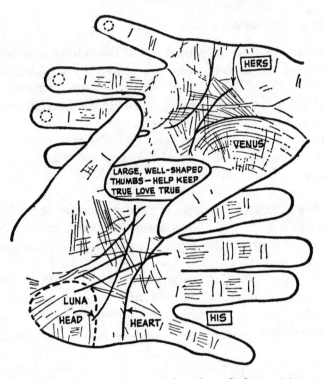

These hands show imagination by their bulging Mounts of Luna. His is intensified by diagonal lines and shows active and restless imagination.

OTHER FACTS

A number of vertical or horizontal lines on the Mount of Luna indicate restlessness and a desire to travel. Traditionally, each is supposed to represent a voyage—vertical lines, a sea voyage; horizontal lines, a trip by land.

THE VIA LASCIVIA

A line across the Mount of Luna emphasizes sensitivity and restless imagination. If it crosses into the Mount of Venus, it shows a desire to escape. It is often found on the hands of the creative artist whose escape into his own imagination is translated into fiction or painting. It got its

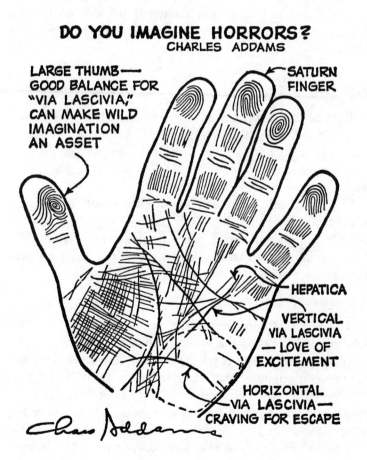

DO YOU IMAGINE HORRORS?
CHARLES ADDAMS

LARGE THUMB — GOOD BALANCE FOR "VIA LASCIVIA," CAN MAKE WILD IMAGINATION AN ASSET

SATURN FINGER

HEPATICA

VERTICAL VIA LASCIVIA — LOVE OF EXCITEMENT

HORIZONTAL VIA LASCIVIA — CRAVING FOR ESCAPE

unfortunate name because it is also found on the hands of people who escape in less acceptable ways.

Another line parallel to the hepatica or health line is called the "Via Lascivia" by some authors. This line emphasizes nervous energy when well marked and usually goes with a love of excitement. Tortuously marked, it belongs to the over-excitable person who may easily become dissipated.

The Via Lascivia is best balanced by a large thumb. With such a thumb, in a well-marked hand, it emphasizes the artistic gift.

THE "MOONLIT" SIDE

Roughly speaking, the area of your hand from the thumb to the middle finger shows power for action and observation. The area between your middle and little fingers reveals the extent of your ability to feel, perceive and dream and sometimes sense things instinctively.

If your middle or Saturn finger leans at all, it slants toward the side of your hand that is most important in your life. In a practical hand, for example, when the middle finger leans toward your smallest digit, you have intuitive business acumen.

THE LINE OF INTUITION

The line that emphasizes the "moonlit" or intuitive side of the hand is called the line of intuition.

If you have a well-marked, curving line from Mercury to Luna, it suggests that your intuition is so strong that you probably possess some form of extra-sensory perception. A square-handed person with this line probably has strong hunches. If your hand is slightly long with conic or pointed fingers, you may even have prophetic dreams.

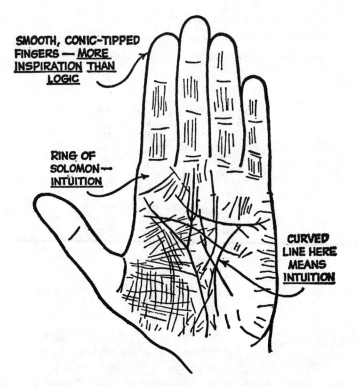

SMOOTH, CONIC-TIPPED FINGERS — <u>MORE INSPIRATION THAN LOGIC</u>

RING OF SOLOMON — <u>INTUITION</u>

CURVED LINE HERE MEANS <u>INTUITION</u>

Curved intuition line under the little finger is seconded by other signs of intuition.

THE HEPATICA

A more or less straight line that slants up the side of the hand from the life-line to Mercury or from Luna to Mercury is called the Hepatica or line of health. It is a sign of good health whether it is clearly marked or non-existent. When badly marked, it suggests sensitive nerves or an improper diet.

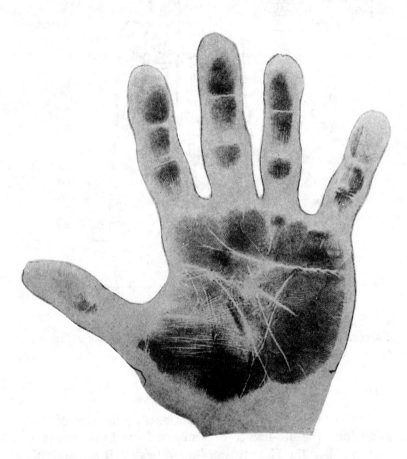

Many talented performers like ballet star Edward Villella have a diagonal fate line beginning on the Mount of the Moon. Hence, the traditional reading: Success by pleasing the whim of the public. You'll find the same kind of fate line in the hands of Helen Hayes. (Original length of print 6-1/2 inches)

CHAPTER XVII

COMBINED MOUNTS

"The whole is more than the sum of the parts."

When certain mounts combine so that a section of the hand is emphasized, a special meaning is added.

We mentioned that the thumb side of the hand is related more to action, the little-finger side to perception. If the Mounts of Venus and Moon combine to emphasize the base of the hand, we have instinctive warmth and instinctive, earthy imagination. These usually combine to make for love of luxury, instinctive originality and spontaneity. It has been called the area of the instincts.

The two Mounts and Plain of Mars form another stripe across the hand. If it is the most developed part of your hand, you have a lot of practical "drive."

If your finger mounts are the most developed section of your hand, your mental energy is the key to your development. If your hand is broadest here, you have intellectual originality.

If your fingers are nearly as long as your palm, they emphasize the finger mounts even if these are not high or wide, particularly in a long hand. A hand shaped this way suggests the abstract thinker, especially if the fingertip

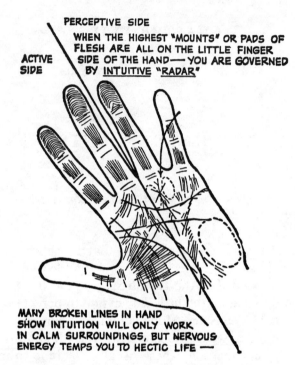

PERCEPTIVE SIDE

WHEN THE HIGHEST "MOUNTS" OR PADS OF
FLESH ARE ALL ON THE LITTLE FINGER
ACTIVE   SIDE OF THE HAND—YOU ARE GOVERNED
SIDE   BY INTUITIVE "RADAR"

MANY BROKEN LINES IN HAND
SHOW INTUITION WILL ONLY WORK
IN CALM SURROUNDINGS, BUT NERVOUS
ENERGY TEMPS YOU TO HECTIC LIFE —

*Most developed side of the hand shows whether you are more
active or perceptive. The lines show how best to follow your
natural bent.*

sections are long in comparison with the other sections.
If in addition you have smooth, conic or pointed fingers,
you may be such an idealist that you are constantly upset
by the cold, hard realities of life.

The highest mounts or those with the most markings do
not always form a large continuous area.

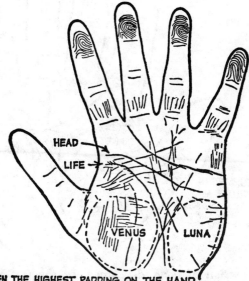

WHEN THE HIGHEST PADDING ON THE HAND
IS ACROSS THE BASE IT SHOWS YOU ARE
SENSUOUS, IMPULSIVE AND HAVE STRONG
BASIC INSTINCTS —

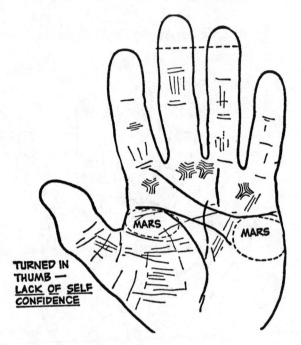

Middle section of hand developed, or the two mounts and plain of Mars in a good hand, show practical push. Other signs—a bent-in thumb, for instance—may show that the ability to push ahead is limited by other character traits.

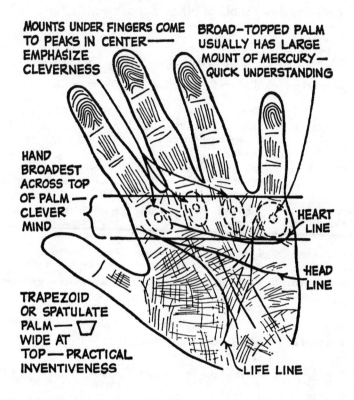

MOUNTS UNDER FINGERS COME TO PEAKS IN CENTER—— EMPHASIZE CLEVERNESS

BROAD-TOPPED PALM USUALLY HAS LARGE MOUNT OF MERCURY— QUICK UNDERSTANDING

HAND BROADEST ACROSS TOP OF PALM — CLEVER MIND

HEART LINE

HEAD LINE

TRAPEZOID OR SPATULATE PALM — WIDE AT TOP — PRACTICAL INVENTIVENESS

LIFE LINE

the top third of the palm is broadest, it emphasizes intellec-
tal originality.

Here is a brief table of other mount combinations:

Most-Emphasized Mounts	Best Results	What to Beware of
Jupiter, Saturn	Wisdom in leadership or ambition in serious studies	Gloomy pride
Jupiter, Apollo	Style and ambition lead to development and use of talents	A desire to show off
Jupiter, Mercury	Ambition plus practical cleverness yield worldly success	Schemes to gratify personal pride, one-upmanship
Jupiter, Passive Mars	Ambition not easily discouraged	Inability to understand and sympathize with weaker souls
Jupiter, Luna	Enough ambition to use imagination creatively	Pride inflated by impossible dreams of glory
Jupiter, Venus	Outgoing, constructive ambition—humanitarian goals	Ostentatious generosity to inflate your pride
Jupiter, Active Mars	Aggressive ambition which lets nothing stand in its way	Tendency to pick fights
Saturn, Apollo	Talent used in a serious way	Gloom that inhibits self-expression
Saturn, Mercury	Serious understanding plus clever self-expression	Temptation to forget scruples because of skepticism about human race
Saturn, Luna	Studious and imaginative qualities of the "deep" thinker	Restlessness and black moods, strange ideas
Saturn, Venus	Kindness and dependability	Pessimism
Saturn, Active Mars	Love of outdoor life	Active grumbling and discouragement that makes action seem useless
Saturn, Passive Mars	Adherence to convictions	Gloom
Apollo, Mercury	Clever use of talent	Pretense and affectation

Most-Emphasized Mounts	Best Results	What to Beware of
Apollo, Passive Mars	Style and endurance — a winning combination	Ostentation
Apollo, Luna	Interpretive or creative talent	Squandered talent, lack of serious purpose, "temperament"
Apollo, Venus	Love of beauty and ability to create it. Music	Tendency not to plan ahead
Apollo, Active Mars	Ability to promote your own talents	Sense of self-importance and habit of sponging on others
Mercury, Passive Mars	Refusal to give up	Tendency to quibble
Mercury, Luna	Ingenuity — practical use of imagination	Fast talk—twisting the truth
Mercury, Venus	Cleverness, vivaciousness, warm-heartedness	Impetuosity
Mercury, Active Mars	Great business ability	Over-aggressiveness
Luna, Passive Mars	Ability to turn dreams into realities	Coldness
Luna, Venus	Energy and originality	Impulsiveness, restlessness and sensuality
Luna, Active Mars	Ability to do unusual out-of-the-ordinary things successfully	Struggle for impossible goals you have dreamed up
Venus, Passive Mars	Tolerance and sympathy, huge physical reserves of energy	Sympathy that is easily exploited by others
Venus, Active Mars	Loyalty and the determination to fight for ideals	Emotionalism
Active, Passive Mars	Great forcefulness	Too much aggressiveness

CHAPTER XVIII

ACCIDENTAL SIGNS

"Awareness of danger brings good fortune."
—I Ching.

How could there be any meaning to anything as coincidental-seeming as a star, a cross or a triangle in a certain part of the hand? The answer is that such signs aren't coincidental.

Groups of lines are found on those parts of the hand that indicate your most-developed qualities. If you use your hand surely and deftly, the groups of lines tend to be clearly marked in a balanced way, as in a well-formed star or triangle. In the hands of an awkward person, the lines have a scrambled and uncertain look.

In an uncertain hand, groups of lines tend to form a grill—an unfavorable sign. In hands covered with lines, single signs don't have much meaning unless they stand out clearly. The squares on your hand are protective signs that are supposed to shield you from possible disaster. For example, a square on the Mount of Jupiter suggests protection against the adverse effects of pride and the thirst for power.

In general, you find square markings on the hands of people who exercise a great deal of intuition in recognizing and escaping serious dangers. This is true even if these people are not intuitive in other ways.

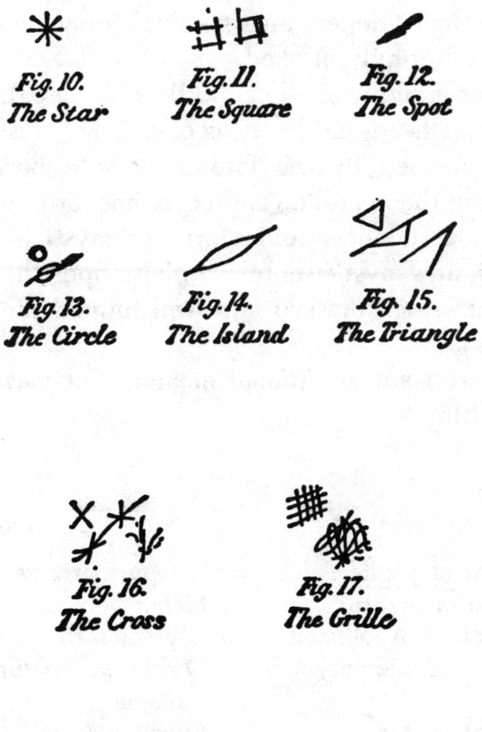

Fig. 10.
The Star

Fig. 11.
The Square

Fig. 12.
The Spot

Fig. 13.
The Circle

Fig. 14.
The Island

Fig. 15.
The Triangle

Fig. 16.
The Cross

Fig. 17.
The Grille

Signs found in the Hand.

An old picture showing common hand-markings (including
a circle, traditionally believed to show dangerous brilliance).

CROSSES

By and large, it seems best to read crosses quite simply as well-marked or badly marked lines on the mount where you find them—depending, of course, on whether they are clear or falteringly marked.

A cross roughly in the middle of the palm, between the lines of head and heart, is called the Mystic Cross. It may be formed by the fate-line and a horizontal line connecting the head-line and heart-line, or it may be quite separate. It denotes some form of mysticism—anything from religious mysticism to just plain.superstition, depending on how well marked and well formed the rest of the hand may be.

Here are some *traditional* meanings of various crosses, just for fun:

Cross	*Meaning*
On Mount of Jupiter:	Happy marriage.
On Mount of Saturn:	Melancholy mysticism.
On Mount of Apollo:	Obstacles to artistic success.
On Mount of Mercury:	Dishonest nature; kleptomania.
On Mount of Mars:	Enemies.
On Mount of the Moon:	Exaggeration, self-deception.
At end of life-line:	Happy old age.
On Mount of Venus:	A single, tragic love.
On lowest section of index finger:	Lewdness.
On lowest section of ring finger:	Chastity.

STARS

Here is what stars mean when they appear on various mounts:

Star	Meaning
On Jupiter.	Great ambition, usually leading to proportionate success.
On Saturn:	Fatalistic view of life, probably gloomy moods. Scholarly success.
On Apollo:	Dash and sense of style, often leading to fame or wealth.
On Mercury:	Talent for science or commerce, or eloquence.
On Luna:	Soaring imagination, hence (traditional reading) fame won through imagination.

And, just for fun, here are some of the *traditional* meanings:

Star	Meaning
On lines circling wrist:	Inheritance.
On Passive Mars:	Honor through fortitude.
On Luna:	Shipwreck.
In center of quadrangle (in a man's hand)	Ruin by a woman; losses recouped.
On tip of Saturn finger:	Danger.
On tip of other fingers:	Good luck in anything you touch.
On tip of thumb:	Success through strong will.
At base of thumb:	Troubles caused by women, or fall from a ladder.
On Mount of Venus:	Success in love affairs.
At end of life-line:	Wealth in old age.

GRILLS

A grill or network of criss-crossed lines on a mount shows so much nervous energy that it is almost bound to be destructive. The more tangled the lines are, and the more they wriggle like swimming snakes, the more the grill suggests self-destructive tendencies.

If a hand is covered with a network of fine lines, don't consider there is a grill on every mount. Take another look at the tables of general line meanings in Chapter VI. To have its strongest connotations, a grill must stand out clearly in the hand.

A firm hand and a large thumb may help you control the unfortunate leanings shown by a grill: so strange and complicated is human nature that, under some circumstances, our very faults can be useful.

For example, a grill on the Mount of Saturn indicates fits of depression. You often see this grill in the hands of a humorist or comedian whose sense of humor has been developed to offset his tendency to feel depressed. In private, however, he will still have blue moods.

A grill on the mount of Apollo shows a desire to show off. In a hand with many twisted lines and a small thumb, this would amount to vanity. On the other hand, you will often see this grill on the hands of successful actors and actresses. Because such people have talent, their way of showing off is pleasing to us and profitable to them.

A grill on the Mount of Venus is very common and shows a need for affection.

GOT A DRAMATIC FLAIR?
"SCHULTZY"

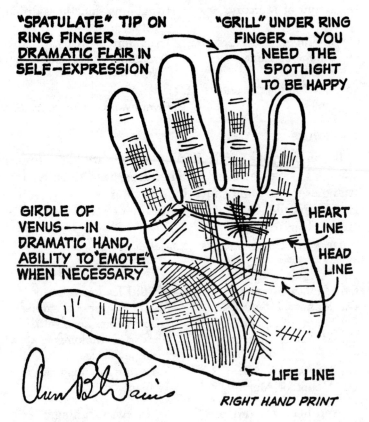

"SPATULATE" TIP ON RING FINGER — DRAMATIC FLAIR IN SELF-EXPRESSION

"GRILL" UNDER RING FINGER — YOU NEED THE SPOTLIGHT TO BE HAPPY

GIRDLE OF VENUS — IN DRAMATIC HAND, ABILITY TO "EMOTE" WHEN NECESSARY

HEART LINE

HEAD LINE

LIFE LINE

RIGHT HAND PRINT

Many actors and actresses who feel at home in the public eye have a grill under the ring finger.

Here are some other grill meanings:

Grill	Meaning
On Mount of Jupiter:	Destructive pride.
On Mount of Mercury:	Instability, sometimes dishonesty.
On Mount of Passive Mars:	Irritability.
On Mount of Luna:	Overactive imagination; constant worry.
In quadrangle (center of palm):	Overawareness of difficulties.

TRIANGLES

If you use your hands deftly, the lines are likely to form triangles, small and large. Therefore, traditionally, most triangles in the hand show some form of skill or good luck. It is an excellent sign if the main lines of the hand make a large, clear triangle.

Here are the meanings of smaller triangles:

Triangle	Meaning
On Mount of Jupiter:	Skillful leadership, tact.
On Mount of Saturn:	Talent in serious studies.
On Mount of Apollo:	Inspired craftsmanship.
On Mount of Mercury:	Shrewd diplomacy; wit; money sense.
On Mount of Luna:	Wise use of imagination.
On Mount of Mars:	Probably calm in crisis.

And here, for fun, are the *traditional* meanings:

Triangle	Meaning
On Mount of Venus:	Calculating in matters of love.
At end of life-line:	A wagging tongue.
On lines around wrist:	A rich marriage.
At end of head-line:	Power of divination.
On Mount of Saturn:	Skill in black magic.

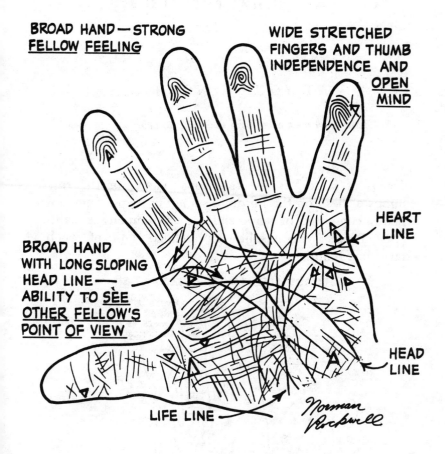

BROAD HAND—STRONG
FELLOW FEELING

WIDE STRETCHED
FINGERS AND THUMB
INDEPENDENCE AND
OPEN
MIND

HEART
LINE

BROAD HAND
WITH LONG SLOPING
HEAD LINE—
ABILITY TO SEE
OTHER FELLOW'S
POINT OF VIEW

HEAD
LINE

LIFE LINE

*Notice how many triangles are formed by the lines in the
skillful hands of artist Norman Rockwell.
(Original length of print 7-1/8 inches)*

CHAPTER XIX

AT YOUR FINGERTIPS

"Better thou wert never born than on a Friday pare thy horn."
—Old jingle.

"Drops of water" is the traditional name for the tiny bumps of flesh on the inside of some fingertips. They are mainly composed of nerve-endings and emphasize sensitivity. People with a subtle and refined sense of touch have such bumps.

DO YOU LIKE TO CRITICIZE?

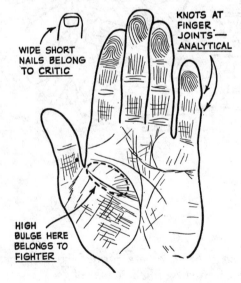

WIDE SHORT NAILS BELONG TO <u>CRITIC</u>

KNOTS AT FINGER JOINTS— <u>ANALYTICAL</u>

HIGH BULGE HERE BELONGS TO <u>FIGHTER</u>

FINGERNAILS

Here are some more clues to character right at your fingertips:

Short nails that are slightly broader than they are long—you crave activity.

Very short nails—you are irritable (or are you a critic?).

Long nails—you are shy with an even temper.

Vertically ridged nails—you suffer from nervous irritability, sometimes because of a run-down condition.

Strong horizontal ridge, especially in the thumb-nail—this often results from a nervous or physical shock in the past—one that has taken place within the last six months, since that is how long it takes the nail to renew itself.

Hard nails—a sign of vigor.

OLD TRADITION

White spots on the nails are a sign of good luck.

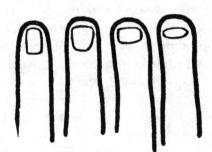

These fingernails show (l. to r.) shyness, frankness, activity, criticism.

CHAPTER XX

FINGERPRINTS AND SUCH

"Fingerprint figures that whirl around in a circle are the 'whirl-pool type' and those running in a water-course are the 'stream type.' . . . Figures and combinations of fingerprints actually tell the fortune of a person's entire life."
—Yusuke Miyamoto, 1963.

The ancient Chinese believed that thumb-print patterns composed of closed circles showed a more focused and powerful mind than prints made up of arches and loops. A Japanese fortune-telling system equates the circle or near-circle fingerprint with the *yang*, or active, male, creative principle, and all other prints with the *yin*, or passive, female principle. Hindu hand-readers believe that a circle pattern on palm or sole is a sign of talent. The science of dermatoglyphics also involves the study of these circular and related spiral prints, or whorls, and the facts scientists have discovered provoke interesting questions.

Why, for example, do men tend to have more whorls on their fingers than women? Why do North American Indians, Chinese, Japanese, Jews and Arabs, for example, tend to have more whorls on their fingers than Dutchmen, Norwegians, Britons or African bushmen? (Readers who want to know more about dermatoglyphics may want to

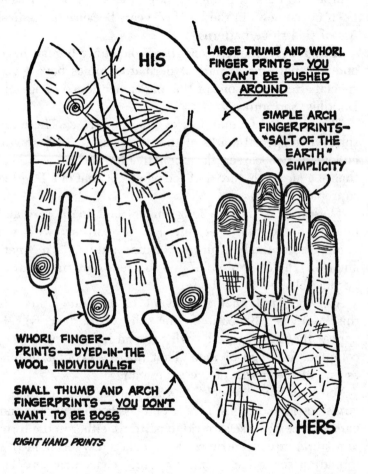

HIS

LARGE THUMB AND WHORL FINGER PRINTS — <u>YOU CAN'T BE PUSHED AROUND</u>

SIMPLE ARCH FINGERPRINTS— "SALT OF THE EARTH" SIMPLICITY

WHORL FINGER— PRINTS — DYED-IN-THE WOOL <u>INDIVIDUALIST</u>

SMALL THUMB AND ARCH FINGERPRINTS — <u>YOU DON'T WANT TO BE BOSS</u>

RIGHT HAND PRINTS

HERS

read *Finger Prints, Palms and Soles,* by Cummins and Midlo.)

Some readers may want to stop at this point and learn a little extra about papillary ridge markings, which have been in the news in the last few years because of medical use of skin ridge patterns.

Intriguingly, modern scientists who study human hand and foot patterns as part of dermatoglyphics have given special attention to one of the marks mentioned in age-old Buddhist scriptures:

"The Exalted One addresses the monks. . . . There are thirty-two special marks of the superman . . . wherewith endowed, two careers lie open to him and none other: that of a monarch, turner of the wheel . . . that of a Buddha supreme."

These marks include long fingers and toes, "soft and tender" hands and feet, physical proportions with the "symmetry of the banyan-tree," hands and feet "like a net" and skin "the color of gold" and so "delicately smooth that no dust cleaves to his body."

And the mark that is relevant to dermatoglyphics is this:"Moreover, beneath on the soles of his feet, wheels appear thousand-spoked, with tire and hub, in every way complete and well divided. That this is so counts to him as one of the marks of the superman."

You may have "wheels" in your hands. The tiny papillary skin-ridge designs have been classified into types and named. One of these skin-ridge patterns, either in the form of a spiral or concentric circles is called a whorl, and this formation seems, in its most perfect concentric circular form, to be the wheel called one of the thirty-two marks of the superman. It is still widely used in oriental fortune-telling.

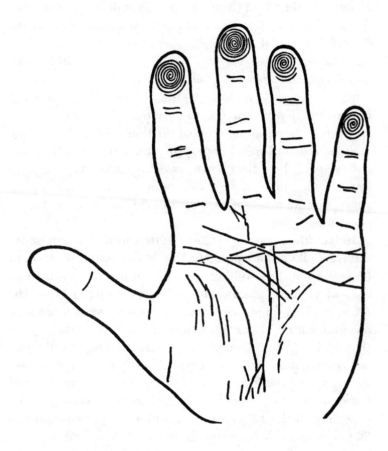

If, like Senator Wayne Morse's hand, yours has whorl finger-prints on all fingertips, it shows forceful character even if the tip section of the thumb (the will section) is short. You will think for yourself and not care whether other people agree.

One modern system of reading from fingerprint whorls is oversimplified until it is like a child's counting-out rhyme. This Indian method says that one lone circle fingerprint out of ten prints means you are clever; two, good looking; three, you love luxury; four, you will be very poor; five, you are well-educated; six, clever even among scholars; seven, a recluse; eight, dirt-poor; nine, a king; ten, you will work for the government.

A more common type of whorl than the perfect circle is the spiral, and spiral fingerprints have their reading too: one, you will be a Raja; two, a wealthy man; three, a yogi; four, a poor man; five, a rich man; six, a yogi; seven, a very poor man; eight, a rich man; nine, a yogi; ten, a poor man.

Indian ideas spread to China with Buddhist missionaries after 217 B.C., and possibly this is the origin of another fingerprint fortune-telling system, still in use, keyed to an ancient Chinese philosophy and fortune-telling book, the *I Ching*. This fingerprint-reading system seems more serious and a little closer to modern ideas. This is the system that calls either the circle or the spiral fingerprint *yang* or creative masculine principle. All other fingerprints are then *yin* or yielding, receptive, feminine. Masculine and feminine are not used here to tell merely what is to be expected on the fingerprints of a man or a woman, for in fact a woman is occasionally seen who has all *yang* or "masculine" fingerprints, a man with all *yin* or "feminine" fingerprints. In the *I Ching* and related Chinese philosophies, the masculine and feminine are used to suggest the two polar forces of the universe that are needed to complete each other. You read a man's left hand or a woman's right hand. The no-whorl hand is the completely yielding, receptive hand. Says the oriental reading: men and women with no-whorl hands, "grow old in peace and comfort just as a huge tree with increasing annual rings."

At the opposite extreme, the all-whorl hand has concentric circles or a spiral in every fingerprint. The oriental
reading calls the owner like a "lone tree in the middle of
a plain"—proud, self-respecting, outspoken and self-made.
Even the more common hand with whorl prints on all
fingers except the thumb has a strong reading: "He must
push and progress with intensity . . . (and) is predestined
to live his life with thrill and strength."

The oriental system reads thirty-two possible fingerprint combinations. I have not studied and used this system so thoroughly that I can say whether I think it all
works. The all-whorl hand has, however, in my experience
always belonged to a strong individualist, whether it be
a leader or an anarchist, and the no-whorl hand usually
belongs to a more flexible person. But the intriguing fact
is that not only Buddhist scriptures but oriental fortune-
telling still in use finds the whorl-marking means something out of the ordinary. And so do scientists.

It was a whorl near the heel of his own hand, a marking he noticed was more common on the paws of monkeys
than the palms of his friends and acquaintances, that
piqued the curiosity of Francis Haythorn Wilder, a biologist, in the late 1800s. He studied the paw-prints of
monkeys galore and took the palm and foot prints of
groups of European descent, Maya Indians, Chinese and
Negroes, studied duplicate twins and other groups to see
what sort of prints were typical of each.

And Wilder wasn't the only scientist studying hand-
markings. As interest grew, identification experts, anthropologists, geneticists, zoologists and anatomists all contributed to the growing store of statistical knowledge
about hand and foot markings.

Now, if you find a whorl on your right ring finger, you

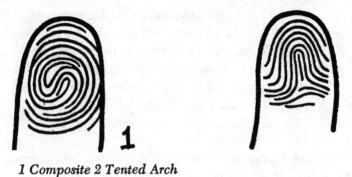

1 Composite 2 Tented Arch

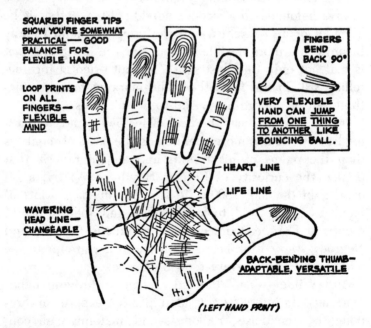

SQUARED FINGER TIPS SHOW YOU'RE SOMEWHAT PRACTICAL — GOOD BALANCE FOR FLEXIBLE HAND

LOOP PRINTS ON ALL FINGERS — FLEXIBLE MIND

FINGERS BEND BACK 90°

VERY FLEXIBLE HAND CAN JUMP FROM ONE THING TO ANOTHER LIKE BOUNCING BALL.

HEART LINE

LIFE LINE

WAVERING HEAD LINE — CHANGEABLE

BACK-BENDING THUMB — ADAPTABLE, VERSATILE

(LEFT HAND PRINT)

The flexible mind, shown by loop fingerprints, can be under-lined by other markings. This hand shows a mind flexible to a fault.

can know that, statistically, this is one of the most usual places for a whorl to be. (Thumbs and ring-fingers are more whorled than other fingers, the right hand more whorled than the left.) If there is a whorl on your little finger, however, this is rarer. Little fingers are most often tipped with loops.

If there are no whorls or few whorls on your fingers, you can know that this is slightly more usual if you are a woman. Women have fewer whorls and more arches among their fingerprints than men. Intriguingly, this dovetails with the Chinese idea that whorls are *yang*, which is firm and masculine, and all other prints are *yin*, which is female as well as yielding.

One out of every five persons has no whorls on his fingerprints at all. Many others have only a few of these "whirlpool" prints. In fingerprints and toe-prints, many whorls are the exception. A hand with few whorls is quite usual.

It is much rarer to find a whorl in the tiny skin ridges of the palm of your hand, or on the sole of your foot, than to find a whorl in one of your fingerprints. And, to scientists, the rarity of these whorls makes them seem significant. Because whorls are much rarer on human palms and soles than on the elevated pads of monkey's paws, and because whorls are scarcer on the more advanced great apes than on the more primitive smaller monkeys, dermatoglyphic authorities Cummins and Midlo believe they are a mark not of the superman of Buddhist scriptures, but of the primitive.

If you have whorls on your palms and soles, this could leave you—and also Mr. Wilder, who helped start it all— in an uncomfortable position.

Psychiatrist Dr. Charlotte Wolff came to the conclusion

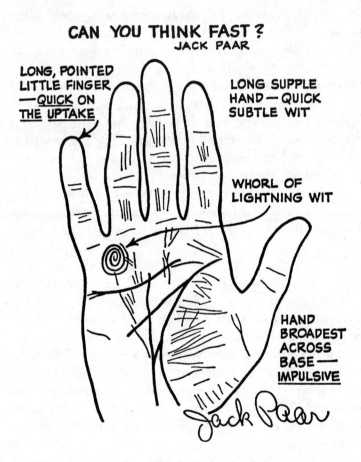

A whorl on the Mount of Mercury shows wit, which is what you'd expect to find on Jack Paar's hand.

that whorls on palms belonged to people with a primitive, atavistic streak in their personalities. Certain families, she believed, tended to produce brilliant off-beat members and subnormal members—not much in the "normal" range in between. Members of these families tended to have whorl on their palms, particularly on the heel of the hand.

Of course, the theories that scientists use to make their findings fit into a meaningful picture can change with new discoveries. But it's interesting that what these scientists gleaned from years of painstaking research is not entirely different from the Buddhist scriptures. The scriptures never said that whorls alone marked a superman, but that they must be one of thirty two marks. And these included long fingers, soft, fine, well-colored skin and beautifully shaped hands and body—and the numerous fine lines typical of sensitive hands.

If whorls indicate the out-of-the-ordinary for better or worse, wouldn't whorled hands and feet with other signs of balance, sensitivity and good health belong to a brilliant original? In my limited experience of the rare hands that approach these standards, the owners have been talented and unique.

Modern British hand-readers who have been interested in character-reading from fingerprints have also come to the conclusion that whorls show strong individuality and originality. The man who has these prints on all his fingers thinks for himself. If you see whorls on certain fingers only, you know their influence is confined to the abilities indicated by these fingers. You'll often find whorls on mounts in the palm, and these signs indicate an intensive and original use of the quality signified by the mount.

The simplest form of fingerprint is called the "simple

arch" and is composed of bent lines like a sergeant's stripes. This arch always reveals a quality of simplicity, often an old-fashioned salt-of-the-earth simplicity. You may find this quality in people of high intelligence. However, people who have these prints on all fingers do •not like to work under pressure.

Modern palmists give meanings to all other types of prints, but I have not found they are as important in interpreting a hand as the two extreme types mentioned above. The others are the loop, which indicates a flexible mind; the tented arch, sign of an idealistic, sometimes artistic mind, and the composite, which symbolizes the ability to see both sides of a question.

CHAPTER XXI

THE PAST

". . . We must respect the past, remembering that once it was all that was humanly possible."
                                    —Santayana.

Why can you read the past in your hands? The oldest theory is that our hands show our horoscopes. Even today, some Indian hand-readers can determine the planets' positions at the time of your birth by studying your hands. V. A. K. Ayer believes that these unusual hand-readers are other-worldly men who cannot entirely explain their methods.

Another theory maintains that our hands reflect whatever we know subconsciously. This is possible if parts of your hand are represented in separate areas of the brain (see Wood Jones' *Principles of Anatomy as Seen in the Hand*) and if detailed memories of the past are stored in specific parts of the brain. Experiments in the stimulation of parts of the brain by electrical impulses tend to support the theory.

In the May 15, 1958, issue of *The Reporter*, Maya Pines said: "Dr. Wilder Penfield, director of the Montreal Neurological Institute, developed a theory that the brain is permanently altered by everything we do. According to him, for each experience we have ever had, there is a corresponding record, like a strip of film ready to be activated by electrical stimulation. Each spot seems to contain only one experience, and always the same one—a moment in one's childhood, a song, a conversation, a dream."

The theory that seems most provable and compatible with other theories might be defined this way: since our hands show what we are, they make it obvious what sort of past we have had. If your hands are full of tortured lines, you have had a lot of troubles.

You can learn more details about your past by comparing your hands. If a line or mount is well marked in the hand you use most frequently and badly marked in the other, you have definitely made progress in mastering your life and realizing your desires and ambitions.

Since the most-used hand is connected with the center of the brain where learned skills are recorded—even such basic ones as talking (see *The Master Hand* by Abram Blau, American Orthopsychiatric Association, 1946)—if the least-used hand is marked much more clearly than the other, your education and training was destructive to the kind of person you were naturally suited to be. Perhaps you had a natural talent for vaudeville but were raised in Boston.

A more clearly defined left hand reveals a right-handed person's possibilities for development; a right hand with clearer markings shows the helpful effect of early training or attempts at self-improvement (maybe you had a temper, but you've learned to control it).

Suppose your least-used hand is flexible, but your most-used hand is stiff. You have become less flexible in your thinking. (The right hand is usually slightly stiffer.)

Suppose your fate-line is badly marked in your active

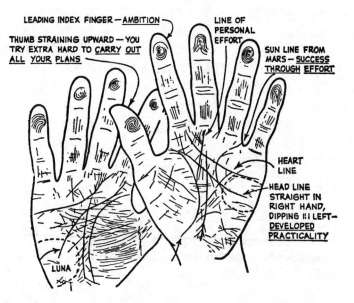

Difference between left hand and right hand show the way you have changed.

hand but well marked in the passive. You have a poor sense of purpose due to improper training or destructive experiences, but you are capable of developing a clearer aim in life (probably your instinctive sense of direction only comes to the fore in emergencies).

Suppose the sun-line is well marked in your most-used hand and badly marked in the other. You have developed a sense of style and perhaps talent as well.

It's fascinating to read your own past because, at the same time, you are taking stock of yourself. If you don't like the direction in which you've been traveling, this is the first step toward changing that direction.

And it's also fun to observe how others are doing and where they are headed.

CHAPTER XXII

READING THE FUTURE

"Of course, it is only by long experience and constant practice that the exact dates, even in the past, can be correctly read, and the most experienced palmist is always liable to make mistakes."

—Mrs. A. Robinson, *The Graven Palm.*

Can you predict the future with absolute accuracy by reading hands? Fortunately, no, though you *can* tell what a man's future is *likely* to be. Even Cheiro, who was somewhat of a fatalist, felt men could alter the future revealed by their hands.

Suppose you undertake to tell the details of a life, past and future, from a hand—not just the general direction, but more exact events.

For example: "Five years ago there was a big change to satisfy ambition. In the 35th year there will be another change because of the conniving of an enemy—but in the long run it will turn out for the best. There will be a brilliant success in the arts before the age of 45" . . . and so forth.

You will find that, in most cases, the subject reports that his past fits your reading. Then, later, the subject usually

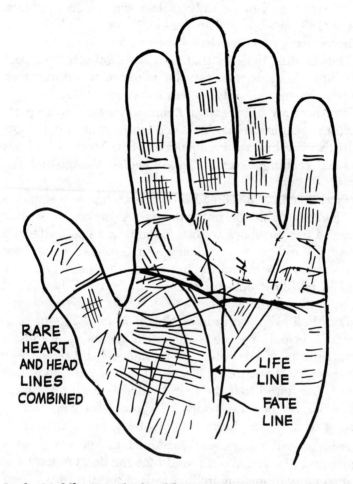

RARE
HEART
AND HEAD
LINES
COMBINED

LIFE
LINE

FATE
LINE

In the Middle Ages the head-line and heart-line combined was read as a sign of an evil life and an evil death. As a matter of fact, the owner of this hand was murdered, but the combined line is by no means a "sign" of murder. Original print tracing: 8¼ inches long. (Original length of print 8-1/8 inches) will report he has been surprised by how exactly the future happened as you said it would.

Clairvoyance may possibly explain some future readings, but it can't possibly explain the fact that certain lines tend to accompany certain events over and over.

The occultist believes that your hand reflects your past and future because it reveals the influence of the stars that largely, but not entirely, determine your actions.

But there are other explanations, for at least some parts of future-reading, that don't necessarily rule out the occultist's view but are independent of it. Modern findings and old readings seem to be connected though not the same.

Traditional palmists read each broken line as a sign of a particular trouble or unhappiness: A broken heart-line means a terrible shock to the emotions or a heart attack; a broken head-line equals damage to the head or at least a breakdown temporarily impairing the intelligence; a broken fate-line means a change—though this last is not necessarily for the worst.

Dr. Wolff kept records of the hand-markings of neurotics, "normal" people, patients in mental hospitals, a number of talented writers, poets, dancers and the like—in other words, both the sick and the healthy, in body and mind. She found that the lines tended to be broken more often in the nervous hands of those who were highly strung or under a physical or mental strain.

Palmists call a long, well-marked fate line a sign of a successful life. Dr. Wolff found that the line tended to be fragmentary or missing in the hands of social misfits or people with little sense of social conscience.

Palmists of the Middle Ages called the line formed by the heart and the head lines joined into one a sign that a man would lead an evil life and come to a bad end.

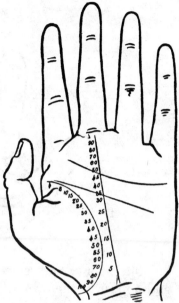

Age, as marked on the life-line and fate-line, as shown in an old palmistry book.

Recently, one of the birth defect clues found by Dr. Achs and Dr. Harper was a heart and head line combined into one line, called the simian line by the scientists. Life must indeed have been "evil" and often short for people with physical defects in the days when there was virtually no treatment for, for example, a malformed heart.

But the simian line is not always a sign of birth defects. It is also sometimes found on people who are apparently entirely normal. The old reading worked—but not exactly, and not always.

My own hunch is that much of future reading from the hands is based on germs of truth—sometimes over-simplified, sometimes exaggerated and sometimes mixed with the most poetic fables. It works well enough to be fascinating but not well enough to be worth the nightmares caused by irresponsible predictions of unavoidable death and catastrophy. Over-simplified traditional readings can sometimes

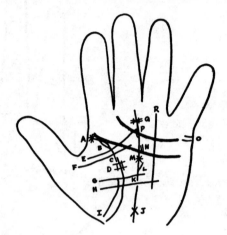

be quite wrong. And remember—hands change; lines fade and appear as the owners' stamina or sense of inner harmony changes.

Yet there is always a fascination in these old readings—and here they are, hopefully to be used with discretion and common sense.

First of all, divide the lines in your hand into ages. An illustration shows how you can indicate various ages on the fate- and life-lines. Make a print or outline of your hand and mark the lines accordingly.

Now trace the course of your life-line from infancy to old age, indicating the traditional meaning of each irregularity:

A star at the very beginning of the line (see A, page 210) is a sign of good fortune in life.

An island on the life-line (B) indicates a period of physical strain.

A break in the life-line (C) means that an illness or shock took place at the time indicated.

A square on the line (D) is a protective sign that

guards you against some threat to your life; if the square is red, you are being protected from fire.

A "worry" line (a line from the Mount of Venus that crosses the life-line) indicates by the lines it cuts what your trouble is all about. You actually began to fret at the point where this line cuts your life-line.

A "worry" line that cuts your heart-line (E) means that you are disturbed by love.

A "worry" line that cuts your head-line (F) indicates that your disturbance can lead to foolish acts.

A "worry" line that cuts your fate-line (G) means that you're worried about money.

A "worry" line that crosses the sun-line (H) concerns your reputation.

A well-marked sister life-line behind the regular line protects you against the troubles marked on the life-line.

Downward branches on any line are traditionally a sign of weakness. The point on the life-line where downward branches begin thus indicates the age when your body begins to weaken. Downward branches on both sides of the life-line mean bad health and many losses. Upward branches are good omens. Branches from the life-line that reach the head-line without cutting it mean riches and honors. A large number of upward branches on the life-line means satisfied ambition and excellent health.

Upward branches are not always read in a cheerful way, however. When they are cut by horizontal or diagonal lines from the Mount of Venus, read them as "law suits." An upward branch cut by a line from Venus to—but not cutting—the Line of Sun means a lawsuit won. But if the upward branch is cut by a line that also cuts the Sun line, it tells of a lawsuit lost. An upward branch cut by a line from Venus to Mercury means divorce.

For every short bar crossing the life line, there will be a

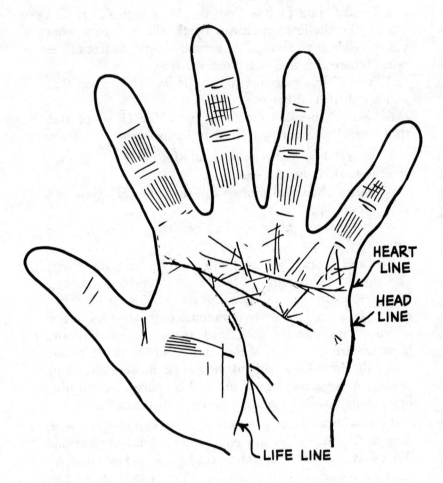

HEART LINE

HEAD LINE

LIFE LINE

Tradition says downward branches are marked on the life-line at the age when vitality begins to lessen.
(Original length of print 8-1/8 inches)

minor illness. For every dot on the line, there will be a minor accident at the age indicated by the position on the line.

Each minor line inside the life-line and parallel to it stands for someone who influences you. The time when he is a force in your life is read by the dates on the part of the life-line each parallels. The importance of the influence is in proportion to the closeness of the influence line to the life-line.

By tradition, a double life-line, in which the inside line begins near the forty-year mark and runs parallel to the life-line like a separate railroad track (I) predicts success followed by exile. Henri Rem says Napoleon III had a line like this.

If your life-line is short, reread Chapter VIII before you get alarmed.

A mole on the life-line announces riches.

The prediction of the future by moles was once known as "moleosophy." A mole on the right hand was supposed to indicate success in business; a mole on the left hand revealed an artistic disposition.

THE FATE-LINE

The fate-line may be lacking in the hand of a go-getter who determines his own fate.

To trace the years on your fate-line, begin at the wrist and work up. (Turn to the illustration on page 209.) Mark the meaning of the line's irregularities on a hand-print.

The most important events of your life *traditionally* happen at a time when your fate-line is most deeply and clearly marked.

A cross on this line is indicative of a change (see J, page 210).

Deep lines that cut the fate-line (G) signify obstacles

"Dukkerin" or Gypsy fortune-tell-
ing signs, placed on houses.

 Go on. Nothing here. They don't believe in fortune telling.

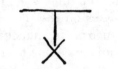 This woman has just had a proposal of marriage.

 Wife here is unfaithful!

 People here have quarrelled over an inheritance.

 Husband here is unfaithful!

Man here is a widower.

Here died an old woman recently.

Very kind people, don't impose on them.

When you tell her fortune, say she will have children, because she wants them.

Woman is a widow.

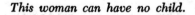 This woman can have no child.

220

that you must overcome.

Breaks in your fate-line (K) indicate changes in your life. If the ends of your fate-line overlap, it means you have switched your course without trouble.

Lines that rise from your fate-line (L) indicate successful projects. A fate-line with many well-marked rising lines forms what hand-readers in India call the "Line of Tree" and is considered a wonderful sign. Gladstone had one.

In the hands of a gambler, a star on the fate-line (M) foretells the date of his losses.

Small lines parallel to the fate-line (N) are signs of good luck and help in meeting challenges on the dates where they are marked. If one of these supporting lines joins the fate-line, marriage is likely. You can confirm this by checking the horizontal line or lines on the edge of your hand just below the little finger (O)—they are the signs of a deep love or marriage.

An island on the fate-line (P) indicates a period of difficulty. French hand-readers say the trouble is the result of a love affair, but others say money is the cause. But your own particular weakness, as shown by the rest of your hand, is likely to be the cause.

If a long-marked fate-line runs high onto the Mount of Saturn, you can expect remarkable good luck throughout your life.

If a well-marked fate-line runs to the Mount of Apollo, your triumph will be artistic.

If a fine fate-line runs to the Mount of Mercury, you will be wonderfully successful in business.

If a beautiful fate-line curves toward the Mount of Jupiter, your worldy ambitions will be fulfilled—perhaps because you will marry well.

But if the line is deep red and runs across the Mount of Saturn and well into the lowest section of the Saturn finger, you will die in a shameful way or go to prison.

The fate-line beginning inside the Mount of Venus tells that your family has ruled your career.

The clear line running from the Mount of Luna to the Mount of Saturn means that your success will be due to the help of someone of the opposite sex.

The fate line ending abruptly at the head-line means that your success in life will be spoiled by poor judgment.

But if it end suddenly at the heart-line, disappointment in love ruins your luck.

One thing you can predict with absolute certainty: if a person has a fate-line with many different markings, his life may be full of ups and downs, but it will never be monotonous.

The dates marked on the sun-line (R) are more or less parallel to those indicated on the fate-line. An island on this line indicates a time in your life when you can't trust to luck or talent but must get what you want by hard work and careful planning.

THE HEAD-LINE

When the head-line twists up and ends on the Mount of Saturn: a fatal head wound.

When the line is very short: early death or loss of mental abilities.

Broken under the Mount of Sun: danger to the eyesight.

Broken under the Mount of Saturn: a head wound, recovery if the ends of the line overlap.

(I have never seen any of these traditional head-line readings come true. But I have seen a very short head-line

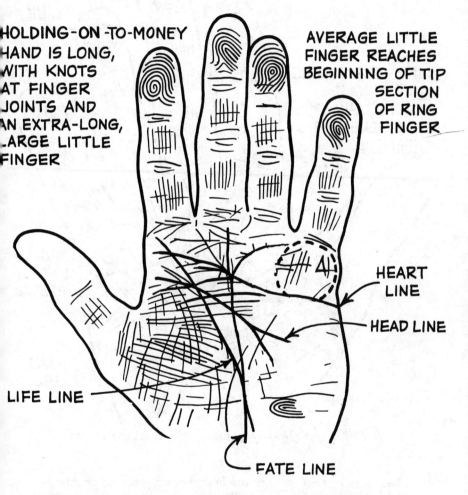

HOLDING-ON-TO-MONEY
HAND IS LONG,
WITH KNOTS
AT FINGER
JOINTS AND
AN EXTRA-LONG,
LARGE LITTLE
FINGER

AVERAGE LITTLE
FINGER REACHES
BEGINNING OF TIP
SECTION
OF RING
FINGER

HEART
LINE

HEAD LINE

LIFE LINE

FATE LINE

*The fate-line to the base of the little finger (Mount of Mercury)
traditionally means you will be brilliantly successful in business. If so the rest of the hand will second the motion.*
(Original length of print 7-1/2 inches)

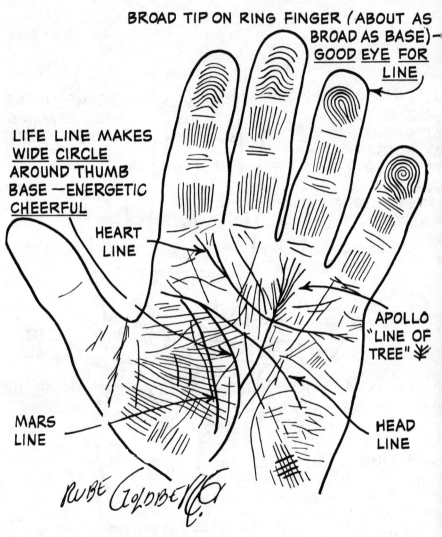

BROAD TIP ON RING FINGER (ABOUT AS BROAD AS BASE)— GOOD EYE FOR LINE

LIFE LINE MAKES WIDE CIRCLE AROUND THUMB BASE —ENERGETIC CHEERFUL

HEART LINE

APOLLO "LINE OF TREE"

MARS LINE

HEAD LINE

RUBE GOLDBERG

The "line of tree" or upward branches on fate-line or Apollo line traditionally means brilliant success; on Apollo, artistic talent too. Notice how the rest of the hand follows suit.

(Original length of print 8 inches)

in the hands of a boy suffering from a serious mental break-down. When he had received treatment and appeared much better, the line lengthened.)

THE HEART-LINE

If the line is chained where it crosses the fate-line, love troubles hurt your career.

The heart-line long and much-branched at the end bodes many minor love affairs. Count the branches—each is a love affair.

Lines drooping from the heart-line under the Mount of Apollo tells of troubles caused by friends.

The heart-line joined to the life-line under the Mount of Saturn means terrible misfortune caused by violent passion.

When many small bars cut the heart-line, repeated disappointments in love are shown.

A break in the heart-line is interpreted differently under each mount. Under Saturn, it says a tragic end to a love affair; under Apollo, a love affair ended by your own inconstancy; under Mercury, a love affair ruined and ended because of greed. If the heart-line overlaps at the point of the breaks, the trouble may be patched up.

All the heart-line breaks are also read as health warnings.

Like the life-line and fate-line, the head-line and heart-line can be dated and used to pinpoint the time of an event. The simplest system is Henri Rem's. He drops a line from the center of each finger.

Here's how he dates the head-line: ten years is marked directly below the index finger; twenty-five years is indicated below the middle finger; fifty below the ring finger

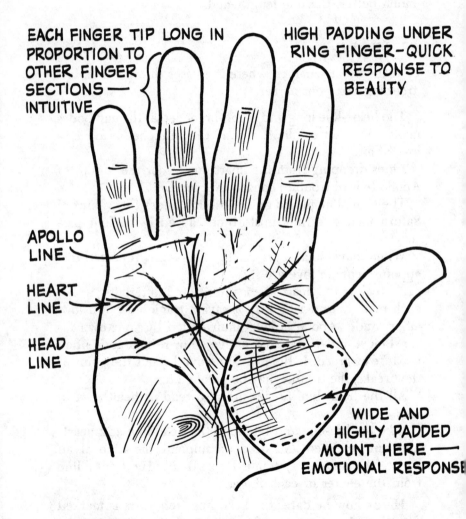

Many branches on the heart-line are read "many love affairs,"
one love for each branch.
       (Original length of print 7-3/4 inches)

and seventy-five below the little finger. Mental strains and difficulties, shown by islands, breaks, cross-lines and pits in the line, are dated according to this system.

He dates the heart-line from the opposite direction—ten years is marked below the little finger; twenty-five below the ring finger, fifty below the middle finger and seventy-five below the index. Heartaches and heartbreaks, shown by islands, breaks and cross-lines, are dated this way.

Nearly every great hand-reader has worked out his own system of reading dates from the lines, but while there is some agreement about dates on the fate- and life-lines, there are so many conflicting systems for the other lines that it seems obvious the fate- and life-lines give more consistent results in dating events.

There is a good, practical reason why dating events on the fate-line in an upward direction gives remarkably accurate results:

When we are young, imagination and animal spirits are usually enough to make us happy and successful. Therefore, if the lines are well-marked in the lowest third of the palm where these qualities are represented, we are likely to do well in early life.

In middle life, we have the greatest need of physical energy and staying power—the qualities represented in the middle section of the palm. When the lines are most clearly marked here, our best years will be between thirty and forty-five.

In our autumn years, it is the quality of our minds that makes the difference. Even if we have not had the push in middle life to be financially successful, we may have acquired a wisdom and philosophy to enjoy our later years. Since our intellectual drives are related to the top third of the palm, well-marked lines here show our chances of success in later life.

And the hand will suggest how to deal with its own special temptations and pitfalls, too. For example, the owner of the pale, hollow hand needs to do everything possible to build himself up, mentally and physically. He needs to be sure of proper diet, medical checkups, healthful exercise and enough pleasant companionship.

The owners of the pell-mell-ambitious and luxury-loving hands can perhaps realize they are spending the coin of life too fast and in self-destructive ways that can leave them bankrupt later. Good qualities, too, are in most hands —perhaps an ability to work hard and pride in a job well done, in an ambitious man; or great generosity in the luxury-lover; or the ability to understand other people's problems in the hollow hand.

Self-knowledge of good qualities as well as bad provides the way to compensate for weaknesses and avoid temptations that future-readings call signs of coming disasters. So, while parts of future-reading are merely points of interest about an interesting old folk-art, other parts may be truly useful.

In regard to periods of "luck" and in other ways, only the character reading that goes with a future reading and explains it makes a hand reading ring true.

For example, a long series of breaks in the fate-line cut by many worry lines suggests a period filled with difficulties. The faults shown in the hands will tell why. Is it because the owner of the pale, hollow hand gives up too easily? Or because the owner of the hand with a high, grilled Jupiter mount is blindly ambitious? Or because the owner of the very soft hand with smooth, fat fingers and a huge Mount of Venus is too extravagant and cares only for luxurious today, forgetting to look out for the future? Probably it is.

CHAPTER XXIII

SUMMING UP

"We say again, and we cannot repeat too often, that a single mark in the hand is not enough to form your opinion . . ."

—Adolphe Desbarrolles.

Beginners at hand-reading are sometimes confused when they find that the same general quality shows in different ways in different hands and that the same quality may be marked in several ways in one hand.

Actually the key qualities to a person's character are always repeated in his hand in a number of ways.

Let's take originality as an example. There are many kinds of originality, and a truly original person can find several varieties marked in his hand. The number of marks and their nature tell us *how* original he is and *in what way*.

If he has whorl fingerprints on most of his fingers, we know he is a person who has to think things out in his own way, a natural-born individualist. If what he does is original, that is just a result of his natural way of thinking.

If he has spatulate fingertips, he is restless, likes to stay busy and is by nature an explorer. He likes to explore places or ideas just because they are new. If he has a

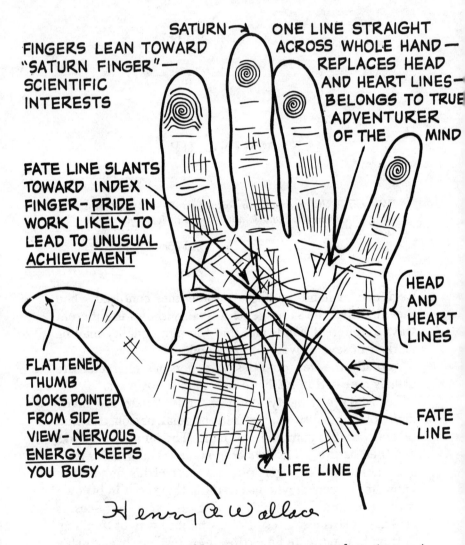

SATURN

ONE LINE STRAIGHT
ACROSS WHOLE HAND—
REPLACES HEAD
AND HEART LINES—
BELONGS TO TRUE
ADVENTURER
OF THE   MIND

FINGERS LEAN TOWARD
"SATURN FINGER"—
SCIENTIFIC
INTERESTS

FATE LINE SLANTS
TOWARD INDEX
FINGER— PRIDE IN
WORK LIKELY TO
LEAD TO UNUSUAL
ACHIEVEMENT

HEAD
AND
HEART
LINES

FLATTENED
THUMB
LOOKS POINTED
FROM SIDE
VIEW— NERVOUS
ENERGY KEEPS
YOU BUSY

FATE
LINE

LIFE LINE

The inventive person like pioneer geneticist and ex-vice-president Henry A. Wallace, will have more than one sign of originality in his hand. (Original length of print 8 inches) spatulate palm too, exploring is his passion; the tried-and-true bore him.

If he holds his thumb and fingers wide apart, we know that he is uninhibited.

If at the same time he has a large and much-lined Mount of Luna, he is extremely imaginative and dreams up exaggerated and unusual ideas.

And on top of all this, if he has an unusual and wild-looking pattern of lines in his hand, you're dealing with an eccentric—a person so out of the ordinary that you are sure he is a genius or a crank or possibly both.

Money-sense also shows in hands in different ways. A long little finger suggests the cleverness to get money, especially if the mount under the finger is high.

If your head-line curves up under the little finger, you are influenced by the desire for money. If the line is fairly straight across the hand, you are practical.

If your fingers are plump enough near the palm so that no light shows through them when you hold them together, you like luxuries and keep yourself supplied with them by holding on to your earnings.

If you have knots on the lower joints of your fingers, you are pragmatic and appreciate money for what it can do for you.

If you have a star or long line under the finger of Apollo, you have style and dash to enable you to make money, though the chances are that you'll spend it freely.

If your little finger is crooked as well as long, you're shrewd. If it's very crooked, watch out! You may be tempted to pull a fast deal.

If your palm and fingertips are square, you are probably basically practical. Along with other signs of practicality in financial affairs, the squareness means that you'll succeed in business.

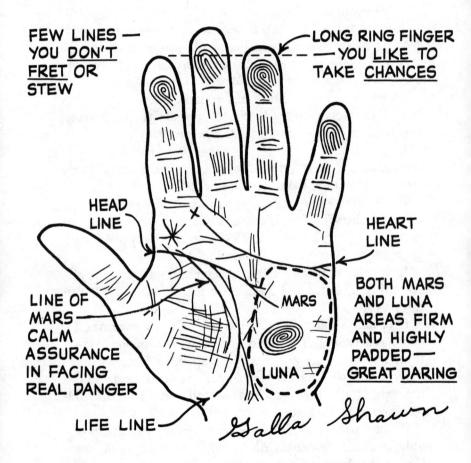

FEW LINES —
YOU <u>DON'T</u>
<u>FRET</u> OR
STEW

LONG RING FINGER
— YOU <u>LIKE</u> TO
TAKE <u>CHANCES</u>

HEAD
LINE

HEART
LINE

LINE OF
MARS —
CALM
ASSURANCE
IN FACING
REAL DANGER

MARS

BOTH MARS
AND LUNA
AREAS FIRM
AND HIGHLY
PADDED —
<u>GREAT DARING</u>

LUNA

LIFE LINE —

Galla Shawn

Any important quality in a hand will be marked in several ways, as daring is repeated in the hand of circus performer, Galla Shawn. (Original length of print 6-3/4 inches)

DO YOU SHOCK PEOPLE?
SALVADOR DALI

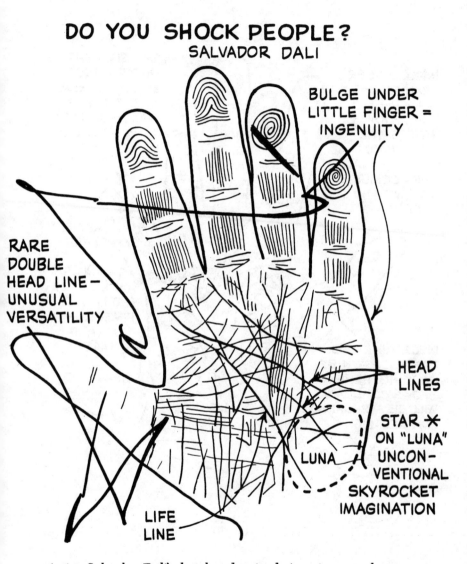

BULGE UNDER LITTLE FINGER = INGENUITY

RARE DOUBLE HEAD LINE — UNUSUAL VERSATILITY

HEAD LINES

STAR ✱ ON "LUNA" UNCON- VENTIONAL SKYROCKET IMAGINATION

LUNA

LIFE LINE

Artist, Salvador Dali's hand makes it obvious in several ways why his art has been a violent shock to some of his contemporaries. (Original length of print 8 inches)

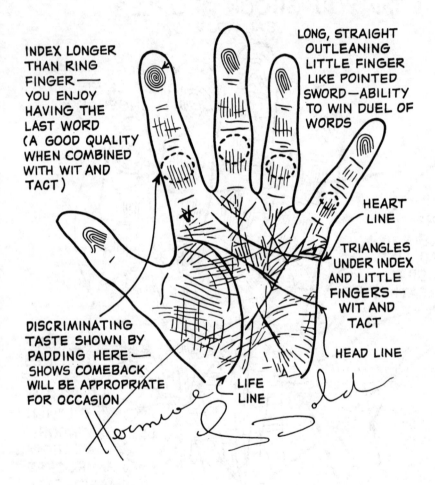

INDEX LONGER
THAN RING
FINGER —
YOU ENJOY
HAVING THE
LAST WORD
(A GOOD QUALITY
WHEN COMBINED
WITH WIT AND
TACT)

LONG, STRAIGHT
OUTLEANING
LITTLE FINGER
LIKE POINTED
SWORD — ABILITY
TO WIN DUEL OF
WORDS

HEART
LINE

TRIANGLES
UNDER INDEX
AND LITTLE
FINGERS —
WIT AND
TACT

HEAD LINE

DISCRIMINATING
TASTE SHOWN BY
PADDING HERE —
SHOWS COMEBACK
WILL BE APPROPRIATE
FOR OCCASION

LIFE
LINE

Quick wit is shown in a number of ways in the hand of Hermione Gingold. (Original length of print 7-1/2 inches)

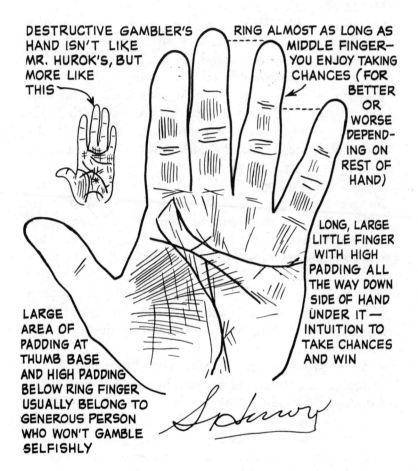

DESTRUCTIVE GAMBLER'S HAND ISN'T LIKE MR. HUROK'S, BUT MORE LIKE THIS

RING ALMOST AS LONG AS MIDDLE FINGER— YOU ENJOY TAKING CHANCES (FOR BETTER OR WORSE DEPENDING ON REST OF HAND)

LONG, LARGE LITTLE FINGER WITH HIGH PADDING ALL THE WAY DOWN SIDE OF HAND UNDER IT — INTUITION TO TAKE CHANCES AND WIN

LARGE AREA OF PADDING AT THUMB BASE AND HIGH PADDING BELOW RING FINGER USUALLY BELONG TO GENEROUS PERSON WHO WON'T GAMBLE SELFISHLY

If an extra-long ring finger suggests that, like impresario S. Hurok, you enjoy taking chances, the rest of your hand will show exactly what kind of "gambler" you are.

(Original length of print 7-3/4 inches)

The person with a large forefinger or a developed Mount of Jupiter is a natural leader who realizes the power of money. These signs are usually indicative of a love for the good life that money can bring.

As you see, you can find endless combinations that describe a man's attitude toward money.

Desbarrolles describes the avaricious hand in this way: the thumb and fingers incline toward each other; the fingers are very square or pointed, stiff, long, thin, dry and knotty; the skin on the back of the hand is hard, dry and wrinkled; the fingers are held together so that no light shows through; the head-line is very straight and forms a bar across the whole hand; the Mount of Venus is flat and feeble; the Mount of Mercury is well developed and grilled, and a large line begins at the short, branched and tortuous heart-line and extends to the little finger.

Warmheartedness also reveals itself in many ways: A high Mount of Venus shows physical vitality and warmth, a long, deep heart-line adds affectionate rapport, and a high Mount of Jupiter further adds a desire to help weaker persons.

A low Mount of passive Mars added to a high Mount of Jupiter in a woman's hand usually signifies shyness and a desire to help others. The woman knows from experience what suffering is. This is especially true if the inside of the fingertips have the sensitivity pads or "drops of water." And a pink hand shows warmheartedness through an overflow of good health.

How about determination? You usually find this quality in a firm hand. (If the person has a long thumb, he may be determined even though he has a soft hand.)

An impulsively wilful person may have a short thumb. This is also true of someone who works well as part of a

DO PEOPLE LISTEN TO YOU?
THIS WEEK — HAL HOLBROOK & MARK TWAIN

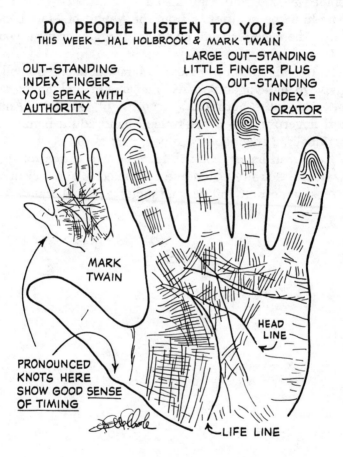

OUT-STANDING
INDEX FINGER —
YOU SPEAK WITH
AUTHORITY

LARGE OUT-STANDING
LITTLE FINGER PLUS
OUT-STANDING
INDEX =
ORATOR

MARK
TWAIN

PRONOUNCED
KNOTS HERE
SHOW GOOD SENSE
OF TIMING

HEAD
LINE

LIFE LINE

*Here are several marks of a talent for public speaking, seen in
the hands of humorist and lecturer Mark Twain, and actor Hal
Holbrook, who is famous for impersonating Mark Twain.*
(Original length of print 8-1/4 inches)

group, though it does not apply to the consistently determined person who plans ahead.

The fate-line or sun-line from the Mount of Mars contributes the necessary will power to struggle for what you want.

The two high, firm Mounts of Mars add energetic willingness to fight against odds. The mount and finger of Jupiter lend the additional incentive of ambition. And whorl fingerprints in a determined hand add a bonus of individualism, the inability to be a part of the herd.

As you read hands, you will learn how to search for the way qualities are repeated and combined to show clearly the most important abilities and motives in each hand.

THE END

BIBLIOGRAPHY

Here is a reading list that will guide you to study any aspect of palmistry that inspires you to dig a little further. Any bookstore can order books in print from the publisher. Others can be found at public libraries or through second-hand book dealers.

PALMISTRY FOR PLEASURE

Bashir, Mir, *How to Read Hands*, Associated Booksellers, Westport, Conn., 1956.

Compton, Vera, *Palmistry for Everyman*, Associated Booksellers, Westport, Conn., 1956.

Hutchinson, Beryl, *Handbook on Hands*, Anchor Press, Tiptree, Essex, England, 1953. Contains a section on handreading vis-a-vis anatomy.

Raymond, Pearl, *Palmistry Explained*, Vista House, New York, 1958.

Van Allen, Rita, *You and Your Hand*, Greystone Press, New York, 1948.

PALMISTRY MORE IN DEPTH: SEVERAL POINTS OF VIEW

Benham, William G., *The Laws of Scientific Handreading*, G. P. Putnam's Sons, New York, 1935.

Cheiro, *You and Your Hand*, Doubleday Doran & Co., New York, 1931. Earlier books on handreading by Cheiro cover roughly the same material but less completely.

Gettings, Fred, *The Book of the Hand*, Paul Hamlyn, Ltd., London, 1965. Beautifully illustrated.

Jaquin, Noel, *Our Revealing Hands*, McBride, New York, 1934.

Rem, Henri, *What Your Hand Reveals*, E. P. Dutton, New York, 1922.

Robinson, Mrs., *The Graven Palm*, Herbert Jenkins Ltd., 1924.
St. Hill, Katherine, *The Book of the Hand*, Rider & Co., London, 1927.
Saint-Germain, Comte C. de, *The Study of Palmistry*, Albert Whitman & Co., Chicago, 1955. Original copyright 1897. Based on the works of Adolphe Desbarrolles.

ACCENT ON PERSONALITY

Laffan, M. N., *Handreading*, Kegan Paul, Trench Trubner, New York, 1932.
Spiers, Julian, *The Hands of Children*, introd. by C. G. Jung, Routledge & Kegan Paul Ltd., London, undated.

VOCATIONS

Benham, William G., *How to Choose Vocations from the Hands*, G. P. Putnam's Sons, New York, 1932.

SOME OLDER PALMISTRIES

Arpentigny, Capt. St. d', *La chirognomie ou l'art de reconnaitre les tendences de l'intelligence d'apres les formes de la main*, Paris, 1853; translated and edited by E. H. Allen, London, 1886.
Belot, Jean C. de Mil-mont, *Sciences de chiromance*, Paris, 1924. Privately printed.
Desbarrolles, Adolphe, *Les mysteres de la main*, Dentu, Paris, 1860; *Revelations completes*, Vigot freres, Paris, re-edition 1922.
Indagine, Jonas, *The Book of Palmestry and Physiognomy*, R. Ibbitson for Ed. Blackmore, Angel in Paul's Churchyard, London, 1656. Earthy—calls little finger the ear-finger because "it is commonly used to make clean the ears."
Metham, John, *Works*, ed. by Hardin Craig, Oxford and Kegan Paul, Trench Trubner, London, 1916. This old English palmistry text, published for the Early English Text Society, is available through the British Book Centre, 122 East 55th Street, New York, N.Y. 10022.

Price, Derek, Jr., ed., *An Old Palmistry*, W. Heffer & Sons, Cambridge, 1953. The earliest known palmistry in English.
Saunders, Richard, *Palmistry—the Secrets Thereof, Etc.*, London 1663.
Steele, Robert, *Introduction and Notes to Secret Secretorum*, (three versions) Anonymous, Early English Text Society extra series, Kegan Paul, Trench Trubner, London, 1898.
Walker, G., *Chiromancy, or the Art of Divination by the Hands*, from a manuscript of 1543, London, 1851.

PALMISTRY AND ASTROLOGY

Baughan, Rosa, *The Influence of the Stars*, Kegan Paul, Trench Trubner, London, 1891. A book of old world lore.
Mihiracharya, *Astro-Palmistry*, Calcutta, 1937.
Sondaz, Marie Louise, *Tous les signes expliques*, R. Laffont, Paris, 1950.

HINDU TRADITIONS

Ayer, V. A. K., *Palmistry for Pleasure and Profit*, Taraporevala Sons & Co., Bombay, undated.
Dale, Mrs. J. B., *Indian Palmistry*, Theosophical Publishing Society, 1895.
Sen. K. C., *Hast Samudrika Shasta, the Science of Hand-Reading Simplified*, Taraporevala Sons & Co., undated.

EGYPTIAN

Gaafar, M. M., *Ilm ul-Kaff* (Science of Hand-Reading), Taraporevala & Sons, undated.

CHINESE AND JAPANESE

Miyamoto, Yusuke, *Fingerprints*, Japan Publications Trading Co., Tokyo, 1963. Readers interested in the I Ching or Book of Changes may like to compare readings and fingerprint patterns in this Japanese system with readings and yin-yang patterns in the I Ching. To make a six-line I Ching pattern comparable to a five-fingerprint hand pattern, two matching central lines are condensed into one.

Soulie, Charles Georges (Soulie de Morant), *Sciences occultes en chine, la main,* Editions Nilsson, Paris, 1932.

GENERAL BACKGROUND AND HISTORY OF HAND-READING

Agrippa Von Nettesheim, *Philosophy of Natural Magic,* ed. by Dr. L. W. de Laurence, published by the editor, Chicago, 1913. Quotation relating rest of book to handreading, page 115.

Ballou, Robert O., ed., *Bible of the World,* Viking, New York, 1939. See especially pages 242-243.

Breuil, Abbe Henri, and Dr. Hugo Obermaier, *Cave of Altamira at Santillana Del Mar, Spain,* Tipografia De Archivos, Madrid, 1935.

Brown, Joseph, ed., *The Sacred Pipe: Black Elk's Account of the Seven Rites of the Oglala Sioux,* University of Oklahoma Press, Norman, Okla. Shows Indian interest in left and right.

Budge, Sir E. A. Wallis, *Amulets and Talismans,* University Books, New Hyde Park, N.Y., 1961.

Clebert, Jean-Paul, *The Gypsies,* tr. by Charles Duff, E. P. Dutton, New York, 1963. Contains translations from Le Journal d'un Bourgeois de Paris, anon., 1405-49, about Gypsy hand-reading. Also excerpt from laws of Manu.

DeCamp, L. Sprague and Catherine, *Spirits, Stars and Spells,* Carnival Press, New York, 1966. For the skeptical.

Hall, Manly Palmer, *Man, the Grand Symbol of the Mysteries,* Philosophers Press, Los Angeles, 1937. Body-reading as part of religion in the 20th Century.

—*The Secret Teachings of All Ages,* Philosophers Press, Los Angeles, 1962.

Luguet, Georges Henri, *The Art and Religion of Fossil Man,* Yale University Press, New Haven, 1930.

Mathison, Richard, *Faiths, Cults and Sects of America,* Bobbs Merrill, Indianapolis, 1960.

Pachter, Henry Maximilian, *Paracelsus, Magic Into Science,* Schuman, New York, 1951.

Paracelsus, *The Hermetic and Alchemical Writings of Paracelsus,* ed. by A. E. Waite, London, 1894.

Peake, Harold, and Herbert John Fleure, *The Corridors of Time*, Vol. 2, Yale University Press, New Haven, 1927.

Spence, Lewis, *An Encyclopedia of Occultism*, University Books, New Hyde Park, N.Y., 1960.

Thorndike, Lynn, *History of Magic and Experimental Science*, Columbia University Press, New York, 1958. The background of hand-reading and examples of its use from an historian's point of view.

Yutang Lin, ed., *The Wisdom of China and India*, Modern Library, New York, 1942. Notice especially pages 383-384.

CLAIRVOYANCE

International Journal of Parapsychology. Parapsychology Foundation, Inc., Eileen J. Garrett president, 29 West 57th Street, New York.

Journals of the American Society for Psychical Research. Published by the society at 5 West 73rd Street, New York.

Pratt, J. G., *Parapsychology, Frontier Science of the Mind*, Charles C. Thomas, Springfield, Ill., 1957.

Rhine, J. B., *The Reach of the Mind*, William Sloane Associates, New York, 1947.

Rhine, Louis E., *E.S.P. in Life and Lab*, Macrʳillan, New York, 1967.

The Journal of Parapsychology, Duke Unive. .cy, Durham, N.C.

SCIENTIFIC POINTS OF VIEW ON HANDS, SOME RECENT, SOME HISTORIC

Achs, Ruth; Harper, Rita, and Siegel, Morris, *Unusual Dermatoglyphic Findings Associated with Rubella Embryopathy*, in The New England Journal of Medicine, January 1966, p. 149.

Bell, Sir Charles, *The Hand, Its Mechanism and Vital Endowments an Evincing Design*, Bridgewater Treatises, No. IV, 1833.

Carus, C. G., *Uber Grand und Bedeutung der verschiendenen formen der Hand*, Verschiedenen Personen, Stuttgart, 1848. Lacking German, I have only read about this one, but it's one of the historical classics.

Cummins, Harold, and Midlo, Charles, *Finger Prints, Palms and Soles—an Introduction to Dermatoglyphics,* Dover Publications, New York, 1961.

Vaschide, N., *Essai sur la psychologie de la main,* Riviere, Paris 1909.

Wolff, Charlotte, *The Hand in Psychological Diagnosis,* Philosophical Library, New York, 1952.

The Human Hand, Methuen & Co. Ltd., London, 1942.

A Psychology of Gesture, Methune & Co. Ltd., 1945.

Wood Jones, F., *The Principles of Anatomy as Seen in the Hand,* Churchill, Ltd., London, 1920.

HAND PRINTS AND ANALYSES

Lindsay, Gertrude Ann, *Your Hand Interpreter and Your Vocation Character Health Analysis,* New York, 1926.

Meyer, Nellie Simmons, *Lion's Paws,* Barrows Mussey, Inc., New York, 1937.

Wolff, Charlotte, *Studies in Hand-Reading,* Alfred A. Knopf, Inc. New York, 1937.

INDEX

O

Occultists, 4, 5, 7, 9, 30, 214
Opportunities, ability to make most of, 8, 39, 51, 111
Orator's hand, 237
Originality, 185, 229, 230

P

Paar, Jack, 206
Paracelsus, 26—27
Penfield, Dr. Wilder, 209
Physiognomy, 20, 22, 23
Pickford, Mary, 31
Position of hand, 42, 49
Praetorius, Johannes, 27

Putnam, 30

Q

Quadrangle, 128-129

R

Ramayana, 18
Rem, Henri, 211
Right hand, 11, 52, 53, 210
Ring of Solomon, 127, 135, 136, 151
Rockwell, Norman, 195
Roosevelt, Eleanor, 46, 142
Rubinstein, Artur, 37

S

St. Germain, Comte C. de, 32
St. Hill, Katherine, 32
Sandburg, Carl, 93
Sanders, Richard, 27
Sargon I, King, liver reading for, 6

Saturn, mount of, 82, 138-140
Saturn, ring of, 161
Sen, K. C., 17
Shaw, Bernard, 47
Shawn, Galla, 232
Sigismund, Holy Roman Emperor, 25, 26
Simian line, 215
Size of hand, 44, 45, 67-70
Skin, papillary ridges, 7, 85—86, 198-208
Skin texture, 46-47, 55, 62
Society for Psychical Research, 31
Spaeth, Dr. Sigmund, 156
Spier, Julius, 27, 32-33
Squares, Persian, 6
    Arab, 6
    protective, 6
    (see also accidental signs)
Steichen, Edward, 14, 15
Stone age, evidence of hand-reading, 5, 16
Susskind, David, 39
Symbols, 1

T

Temper, 168
Temperature of hands, 47, 96
Theosophical Society, 31
Thumb, 51, 61, 71, 80, 83, 93, 97, 101, 103, 109-118, 128, 131, 136, 141, 146, 149, 151, 168, 175, 176, 199, 211, 230
Twain, Mark, 31, 237
Types of hands, 54-70

V

Vaschide, Dr. N., 30
Venus, mount, 82, 99, 102, 106, 107, 113, 217, 235

Via Lascivia, 177-178
Villella, Edward, 180
Vivekananda, Swami, 31

W

Wallace, Henry A., 230
Warm-heartedness, 236
Wilder, Harris Hawthorne, 29, 203. 205

Witty hands, 234, 237
Wolff, Dr. Charlotte, 12, 30, 33, 34, 102, 205, 214
Worry lines, 217

Y

Yang, 202
Yin, 202

MELVIN POWERS SELF-IMPROVEMENT LIBRARY

ASTROLOGY

____ ASTROLOGY: HOW TO CHART YOUR HOROSCOPE *Max Heindel* 5.00
____ ASTROLOGY AND SEXUAL ANALYSIS *Morris C. Goodman* 5.00
____ ASTROLOGY MADE EASY *Astarte* 3.00
____ ASTROLOGY MADE PRACTICAL *Alexandra Kayhle* 3.00
____ ASTROLOGY, ROMANCE, YOU AND THE STARS *Anthony Norvell* 4.00
____ MY WORLD OF ASTROLOGY *Sydney Omarr* 7.00
____ THOUGHT DIAL *Sydney Omarr* 4.00
____ WHAT THE STARS REVEAL ABOUT THE MEN IN YOUR LIFE *Thelma White* 3.00

BRIDGE

____ BRIDGE BIDDING MADE EASY *Edwin B. Kantar* 10.00
____ BRIDGE CONVENTIONS *Edwin B. Kantar* 7.00
____ BRIDGE HUMOR *Edwin B. Kantar* 5.00
____ COMPETITIVE BIDDING IN MODERN BRIDGE *Edgar Kaplan* 4.00
____ DEFENSIVE BRIDGE PLAY COMPLETE *Edwin B. Kantar* 15.00
____ GAMESMAN BRIDGE—Play Better with Kantar *Edwin B. Kantar* 5.00
____ HOW TO IMPROVE YOUR BRIDGE *Alfred Sheinwold* 5.00
____ IMPROVING YOUR BIDDING SKILLS *Edwin B. Kantar* 4.00
____ INTRODUCTION TO DECLARER'S PLAY *Edwin B. Kantar* 5.00
____ INTRODUCTION TO DEFENDER'S PLAY *Edwin B. Kantar* 3.00
____ KANTAR FOR THE DEFENSE *Edwin B. Kantar* 5.00
____ KANTAR FOR THE DEFENSE VOLUME 2 *Edwin B. Kantar* 7.00
____ SHORT CUT TO WINNING BRIDGE *Alfred Sheinwold* 3.00
____ TEST YOUR BRIDGE PLAY *Edwin B. Kantar* 5.00
____ VOLUME 2—TEST YOUR BRIDGE PLAY *Edwin B. Kantar* 5.00
____ WINNING DECLARER PLAY *Dorothy Hayden Truscott* 5.00

BUSINESS, STUDY & REFERENCE

____ CONVERSATION MADE EASY *Elliot Russell* 4.00
____ EXAM SECRET *Dennis B. Jackson* 3.00
____ FIX-IT BOOK *Arthur Symons* 2.00
____ HOW TO DEVELOP A BETTER SPEAKING VOICE *M. Hellier* 4.00
____ HOW TO SELF-PUBLISH YOUR BOOK & MAKE IT A BEST SELLER *Melvin Powers* 10.00
____ INCREASE YOUR LEARNING POWER *Geoffrey A. Dudley* 3.00
____ PRACTICAL GUIDE TO BETTER CONCENTRATION *Melvin Powers* 3.00
____ PRACTICAL GUIDE TO PUBLIC SPEAKING *Maurice Forley* 5.00
____ 7 DAYS TO FASTER READING *William S. Schaill* 3.00
____ SONGWRITERS' RHYMING DICTIONARY *Jane Shaw Whitfield* 6.00
____ SPELLING MADE EASY *Lester D. Basch & Dr. Milton Finkelstein* 3.00
____ STUDENT'S GUIDE TO BETTER GRADES *J. A. Rickard* 3.00
____ TEST YOURSELF—Find Your Hidden Talent *Jack Shafer* 3.00
____ YOUR WILL & WHAT TO DO ABOUT IT *Attorney Samuel G. Kling* 4.00

CALLIGRAPHY

____ ADVANCED CALLIGRAPHY *Katherine Jeffares* 7.00
____ CALLIGRAPHER'S REFERENCE BOOK *Anne Leptich & Jacque Evans* 7.00
____ CALLIGRAPHY—The Art of Beautiful Writing *Katherine Jeffares* 7.00
____ CALLIGRAPHY FOR FUN & PROFIT *Anne Leptich & Jacque Evans* 7.00
____ CALLIGRAPHY MADE EASY *Tina Serafini* 7.00

CHESS & CHECKERS

____ BEGINNER'S GUIDE TO WINNING CHESS *Fred Reinfeld* 5.00
____ CHESS IN TEN EASY LESSONS *Larry Evans* 5.00
____ CHESS MADE EASY *Milton L. Hanauer* 3.00
____ CHESS PROBLEMS FOR BEGINNERS *edited by Fred Reinfeld* 2.00
____ CHESS SECRETS REVEALED *Fred Reinfeld* 2.00
____ CHESS TACTICS FOR BEGINNERS *edited by Fred Reinfeld* 4.00
____ CHESS THEORY & PRACTICE *Morry & Mitchell* 2.00
____ HOW TO WIN AT CHECKERS *Fred Reinfeld* 3.00
____ 1001 BRILLIANT WAYS TO CHECKMATE *Fred Reinfeld* 4.00
____ 1001 WINNING CHESS SACRIFICES & COMBINATIONS *Fred Reinfeld* 4.00
____ SOVIET CHESS *Edited by R. G. Wade* 3.00

COOKERY & HERBS

GAMBLING & POKER

HEALTH

HYPNOTISM

_____ PRACTICAL HYPNOTISM *Philip Magonet, M.D.*		3.00
_____ SECRETS OF HYPNOTISM *S. J. Van Pelt, M.D.*		5.00
_____ SELF-HYPNOSIS A Conditioned-Response Technique *Laurence Sparks*		7.00
_____ SELF-HYPNOSIS Its Theory, Technique & Application *Melvin Powers*		3.00
_____ THERAPY THROUGH HYPNOSIS *edited by Raphael H. Rhodes*		5.00

JUST FOR WOMEN

_____ COSMOPOLITAN'S GUIDE TO MARVELOUS MEN Fwd. by *Helen Gurley Brown*		3.00
_____ COSMOPOLITAN'S HANG-UP HANDBOOK Foreword by *Helen Gurley Brown*		4.00
_____ COSMOPOLITAN'S LOVE BOOK—A Guide to Ecstasy in Bed		5.00
_____ COSMOPOLITAN'S NEW ETIQUETTE GUIDE Fwd. by *Helen Gurley Brown*		4.00
_____ I AM A COMPLEAT WOMAN *Doris Hagopian & Karen O'Connor Sweeney*		3.00
_____ JUST FOR WOMEN—A Guide to the Female Body *Richard E. Sand, M.D.*		5.00
_____ NEW APPROACHES TO SEX IN MARRIAGE *John E. Eichenlaub, M.D.*		3.00
_____ SEXUALLY ADEQUATE FEMALE *Frank S. Caprio, M.D.*		3.00
_____ SEXUALLY FULFILLED WOMAN *Dr. Rachel Copelan*		5.00
_____ YOUR FIRST YEAR OF MARRIAGE *Dr. Tom McGinnis*		3.00

MARRIAGE, SEX & PARENTHOOD

_____ ABILITY TO LOVE *Dr. Allan Fromme*		6.00
_____ GUIDE TO SUCCESSFUL MARRIAGE *Drs. Albert Ellis & Robert Harper*		5.00
_____ HOW TO RAISE AN EMOTIONALLY HEALTHY, HAPPY CHILD *A. Ellis*		5.00
_____ SEX WITHOUT GUILT *Albert Ellis, Ph.D.*		5.00
_____ SEXUALLY ADEQUATE MALE *Frank S. Caprio, M.D.*		3.00
_____ SEXUALLY FULFILLED MAN *Dr. Rachel Copelan*		5.00
_____ STAYING IN LOVE *Dr. Norton F. Kristy*		7.00

METAPHYSICS & OCCULT

_____ BOOK OF TALISMANS, AMULETS & ZODIACAL GEMS *William Pavitt*		5.00
_____ CONCENTRATION—A Guide to Mental Mastery *Mouni Sadhu*		5.00
_____ CRITIQUES OF GOD *Edited by Peter Angeles*		7.00
_____ EXTRA-TERRESTRIAL INTELLIGENCE—The First Encounter		6.00
_____ FORTUNE TELLING WITH CARDS *P. Foli*		4.00
_____ HANDWRITING ANALYSIS MADE EASY *John Marley*		5.00
_____ HANDWRITING TELLS *Nadya Olyanova*		7.00
_____ HOW TO INTERPRET DREAMS, OMENS & FORTUNE TELLING SIGNS *Gettings*		3.00
_____ HOW TO UNDERSTAND YOUR DREAMS *Geoffrey A. Dudley*		3.00
_____ ILLUSTRATED YOGA *William Zorn*		3.00
_____ IN DAYS OF GREAT PEACE *Mouni Sadhu*		3.00
_____ LSD—THE AGE OF MIND *Bernard Roseman*		2.00
_____ MAGICIAN—His Training and Work *W. E. Butler*		3.00
_____ MEDITATION *Mouni Sadhu*		7.00
_____ MODERN NUMEROLOGY *Morris C. Goodman*		5.00
_____ NUMEROLOGY—ITS FACTS AND SECRETS *Ariel Yvon Taylor*		3.00
_____ NUMEROLOGY MADE EASY *W. Mykian*		5.00
_____ PALMISTRY MADE EASY *Fred Gettings*		5.00
_____ PALMISTRY MADE PRACTICAL *Elizabeth Daniels Squire*		5.00
_____ PALMISTRY SECRETS REVEALED *Henry Frith*		3.00
_____ PROPHECY IN OUR TIME *Martin Ebon*		2.50
_____ PSYCHOLOGY OF HANDWRITING *Nadya Olyanova*		5.00
_____ SUPERSTITION—Are You Superstitious? *Eric Maple*		2.00
_____ TAROT *Mouni Sadhu*		8.00
_____ TAROT OF THE BOHEMIANS *Papus*		5.00
_____ WAYS TO SELF-REALIZATION *Mouni Sadhu*		3.00
_____ WHAT YOUR HANDWRITING REVEALS *Albert E. Hughes*		3.00
_____ WITCHCRAFT, MAGIC & OCCULTISM—A Fascinating History *W. B. Crow*		5.00
_____ WITCHCRAFT—THE SIXTH SENSE *Justine Glass*		5.00
_____ WORLD OF PSYCHIC RESEARCH *Hereward Carrington*		2.00

SELF-HELP & INSPIRATIONAL

_____ DAILY POWER FOR JOYFUL LIVING *Dr. Donald Curtis*		5.00
_____ DYNAMIC THINKING *Melvin Powers*		2.00
_____ GREATEST POWER IN THE UNIVERSE *U. S. Andersen*		5.00
_____ GROW RICH WHILE YOU SLEEP *Ben Sweetland*		3.00
_____ GROWTH THROUGH REASON *Albert Ellis, Ph.D.*		4.00

_____ GUIDE TO PERSONAL HAPPINESS *Albert Ellis, Ph.D. & Irving Becker, Ed. D.*	5.00
_____ HELPING YOURSELF WITH APPLIED PSYCHOLOGY *R. Henderson*	2.00
_____ HOW TO ATTRACT GOOD LUCK *A. H. Z. Carr*	5.00
_____ HOW TO BE GREAT *Dr. Donald Curtis*	5.00
_____ HOW TO DEVELOP A WINNING PERSONALITY *Martin Panzer*	5.00
_____ HOW TO DEVELOP AN EXCEPTIONAL MEMORY *Young & Gibson*	5.00
_____ HOW TO LIVE WITH A NEUROTIC *Albert Ellis, Ph. D.*	5.00
_____ HOW TO OVERCOME YOUR FEARS *M. P. Leahy, M.D.*	3.00
_____ HOW TO SUCCEED *Brian Adams*	7.00
_____ HOW YOU CAN HAVE CONFIDENCE AND POWER *Les Giblin*	5.00
_____ HUMAN PROBLEMS & HOW TO SOLVE THEM *Dr. Donald Curtis*	5.00
_____ I CAN *Ben Sweetland*	7.00
_____ I WILL *Ben Sweetland*	3.00
_____ LEFT-HANDED PEOPLE *Michael Barsley*	5.00
_____ MAGIC IN YOUR MIND *U. S. Andersen*	6.00
_____ MAGIC OF THINKING BIG *Dr. David J. Schwartz*	3.00
_____ MAGIC POWER OF YOUR MIND *Walter M. Germain*	5.00
_____ MENTAL POWER THROUGH SLEEP SUGGESTION *Melvin Powers*	3.00
_____ NEW GUIDE TO RATIONAL LIVING *Albert Ellis, Ph.D. & R. Harper, Ph.D.*	3.00
_____ PROJECT YOU *A Manual of Rational Assertiveness Training Paris & Casey*	6.00
_____ PSYCHO-CYBERNETICS *Maxwell Maltz, M.D.*	5.00
_____ SALES CYBERNETICS *Brian Adams*	7.00
_____ SCIENCE OF MIND IN DAILY LIVING *Dr. Donald Curtis*	5.00
_____ SECRET OF SECRETS *U. S. Andersen*	6.00
_____ SECRET POWER OF THE PYRAMIDS *U. S. Andersen*	5.00
_____ SELF-THERAPY FOR THE STUTTERER *Malcolm Fraser*	3.00
_____ STUTTERING AND WHAT YOU CAN DO ABOUT IT *W. Johnson, Ph.D.*	2.50
_____ SUCCESS-CYBERNETICS *U. S. Andersen*	6.00
_____ 10 DAYS TO A GREAT NEW LIFE *William E. Edwards*	3.00
_____ THINK AND GROW RICH *Napoleon Hill*	5.00
_____ THINK YOUR WAY TO SUCCESS *Dr. Lew Losoncy*	5.00
_____ THREE MAGIC WORDS *U. S. Andersen*	7.00
_____ TREASURY OF COMFORT *edited by Rabbi Sidney Greenberg*	5.00
_____ TREASURY OF THE ART OF LIVING *Sidney S. Greenberg*	5.00
_____ YOU ARE NOT THE TARGET *Laura Huxley*	5.00
_____ YOUR SUBCONSCIOUS POWER *Charles M. Simmons*	5.00
_____ YOUR THOUGHTS CAN CHANGE YOUR LIFE *Dr. Donald Curtis*	5.00

SPORTS

_____ BICYCLING FOR FUN AND GOOD HEALTH *Kenneth E. Luther*	2.00
_____ BILLIARDS—Pocket • Carom • Three Cushion *Clive Cottingham, Jr.*	5.00
_____ CAMPING-OUT 101 Ideas & Activities *Bruno Knobel*	2.00
_____ COMPLETE GUIDE TO FISHING *Vlad Evanoff*	2.00
_____ HOW TO IMPROVE YOUR RACQUETBALL *Lubarsky Kaufman & Scagnetti*	3.00
_____ HOW TO WIN AT POCKET BILLIARDS *Edward D. Knuchell*	5.00
_____ JOY OF WALKING *Jack Scagnetti*	3.00
_____ LEARNING & TEACHING SOCCER SKILLS *Eric Worthington*	3.00
_____ MOTORCYCLING FOR BEGINNERS *I. G. Edmonds*	3.00
_____ RACQUETBALL FOR WOMEN *Toni Hudson, Jack Scagnetti & Vince Rondone*	3.00
_____ RACQUETBALL MADE EASY *Steve Lubarsky, Rod Delson & Jack Scagnetti*	4.00
_____ SECRET OF BOWLING STRIKES *Dawson Taylor*	3.00
_____ SECRET OF PERFECT PUTTING *Horton Smith & Dawson Taylor*	5.00
_____ SOCCER—The Game & How to Play It *Gary Rosenthal*	3.00
_____ STARTING SOCCER *Edward F. Dolan, Jr.*	3.00

The books listed above can be obtained from your book dealer or directly from Melvin Powers. When ordering, please remit 50¢ per book postage & handling. Send for our free illustrated catalog of self-improvement books.

Melvin Powers

12015 Sherman Road, No. Hollywood, California 91605